At Issue

Transgender People

Other Books in the At Issue Series:

At Issue

| Transgender People

Roman Espejo, Book Editor

GREENHAVEN PRESS
A part of Gale, Cengage Learning

GALE
CENGAGE Learning™

Detroit • New York • San Francisco • New Haven, Conn • Waterville, Maine • London

GALE
CENGAGE Learning™

Christine Nasso, *Publisher*
Elizabeth Des Chenes, *Managing Editor*

© 2011 Greenhaven Press, a part of Gale, Cengage Learning.

Gale and Greenhaven Press are registered trademarks used herein under license.

For more information, contact:
Greenhaven Press
27500 Drake Rd.
Farmington Hills, MI 48331-3535
Or you can visit our Internet site at gale.cengage.com

LIBRARY OF CONGRESS CATALOGING-IN-PUBLICATION DATA

Transgender people / Roman Espejo, book editor.
    p. cm. -- (At issue)
    Includes bibliographical references and index.
    ISBN 978-0-7377-4896-3 (hbk.) -- ISBN 978-0-7377-4897-0 (pbk.)
    1. Transgender people--Juvenile literature. 2. Gender identity--Juvenile literature. I. Espejo, Roman, 1977-
    HQ77.9.T7159 2010
    306.76'8--dc22
                                                                2010028585

Printed in the United States of America
1 2 3 4 5 6 7 14 13 12 11 10

Contents

Introduction

The prefix "trans" means "beyond," "across," or "over." However, "transgender" does not simply connote a gender that crosses boundaries. It is a broad term, particularly in the lesbian and gay community, to describe individuals whose identity or experience does not fit within the expectations of their birth sex. People with gender identity disorder (GID), transsexuals, cross-dressers, and the so-called genderqueer, are considered to be transgender. Performers such as drag queens and drag kings often are labeled as such, but most do not want to live as the opposite sex and most do not believe they've been "born in the wrong body." (For the same reason, identifying as homosexual and having same-sex attractions is distinct from being transgender.) Furthermore, a person who is born with both male and female biological characteristics is considered to be intersex.

GID and gender dysphoria are terms used by psychologists and in mental health settings. According to the fourth edition of the *Diagnostic and Statistical Manual of Mental Disorders (DSM-IV)*, the criteria for a formal diagnosis are repetitive claims or desires to be the opposite sex and discontent with one's birth sex, intense conflicts with assigned gender roles and behaviors, and impaired social activities and relationships as a result of this distress. (A person who is intersex is excluded from a GID diagnosis, and not all transgender people have gender dysphoria.) A rigorous debate is under way among medical professionals and transgender groups whether GID should no longer be categorized as a mental illness. It may be deleted from the next edition of the *DSM*, which is scheduled to be published in 2013.

A transsexual is a person who changes his or her sex—physically, legally, or both. While most transsexuals undergo sex-reassignment surgery and hormone therapy, not all choose to have medical treatment. "Transitioning" describes transsexuals who are on the course of changing their sex. Common terms for transitioning individuals are male-to-female (MTF) or female-to-male (FTM).

People who habitually wear the clothing, accessories, and cosmetics of the opposite sex are known as cross-dressers. (The word "transvestite" is offensive to some.) As a form of expression, not identity, a cross-dresser does not desire to live permanently as the other gender and may keep such activities private. Erotic or sexual arousal through cross-dressing is called "transvestic fetishism."

Genderqueer is a term used by people who either identify or express themselves as male and female or reject both, claiming that a "third," or other, gender exists. In fact, the third gender appears in numerous cultures, from the "two-spirit" members of several Native American tribes, to the *hijra* of South Asia, to the *mahu* in Polynesian tradition. Some individuals, of all sexual orientations, who transgress the conventions of gender may be labeled as genderqueer.

Gender variance and expression defined in the lesbian and gay community are controversial, with much opposition among conservative and traditional-values groups, which assert that GID is a treatable emotional disorder. "No one can change sex; it is written in DNA on every cell of our bodies," argues Dale O'Leary, a freelance writer and pro-family advocate. "The idea that they were 'transsexual' may have been suggested to them by a mental health professional or they may have seen reports of 'sex changes' in the media. They deceived themselves into believing that this would be the answer to all their problems."[1]

On the other end of the political spectrum, some transgender activists contend that these terms follow an oppressive "cisgender" perspective—people whose gender identity match

1. pfox-exgays.blogspot.com, March 21, 2010, http://pfox-exgays.blogspot.com/2010/03/gender-identity-disorder.html.

their birth sex. "Interestingly very few people seem to see any need to decide what 'biological sex' actually is, given that it has about a million different scientific meanings," a blogger on *Feministing.com* asserts. "Transgender people don't fit into these ideas of gender, so we are dishonest always. I can't say I am female without being accused of lying about my assigned biological sex. And I can't say I'm male, because that isn't my gender identity nor is how I'm usually perceived. . . ."[2]

The complex and varied terminology reveals how gender identity and expression revolve around definition—what being "male" and "female" fundamentally mean. Many transgender men, women, boys, and girls go about everyday life without suspicion. But how they define themselves have consequences for schools, the workplace, public facilities, and sports. *At Issue: Transgender People* explores these individuals' lives and the social, medical, and religious issues that surround them.

2. *Feministing.com*, November 5, 2009, http://community.feministing.com/2009/11/being-transgender-is-dishonest.html.

1

Transgender People Suffer from Gender Identity Disorders

Psychology Today

Founded in 1967, Psychology Today *is a bimonthly magazine focused on psychology and human behavior.*

A person who identifies with the opposite sex and is uncomfortable with his or her assigned sex suffers from gender identity disorder (GID) or transsexualism. Along with the desire to live as a person of the opposite sex, the person may have mannerisms and may dress as the other gender. This is different from homosexuality, in which the person is almost always comfortable with his or her own sex or gender. People with GID are preoccupied with their gender distress and also may suffer from emotional problems. Children may have symptoms of depression or anxiety, adolescents are at risk of depression and suicide, and adults may show signs of depression and anxiety.

Gender identity disorder (GID) or transsexualism is defined by strong, persistent feelings of identification with the opposite gender and discomfort with one's own assigned sex. People with GID desire to live as members of the opposite sex and often dress and use mannerisms associated with the other gender. For instance, a person identified as a boy may feel and act like a girl. This is distinct from homosexuality in that homosexuals nearly always identify with their apparent sex or gender.

Identity issues may manifest in a variety of different ways. For example, some people with normal genitals and secondary sex characteristics of one gender privately identify more with the other gender. Some may cross-dress, and some may actually seek sex-change surgery. Others are born with ambiguous genitalia, which can raise identity issues.

Associated Features and Disorders of Gender Identity Disorder

Many individuals with gender identity disorder become socially isolated, whether by choice or through ostracization, which can contribute to low self-esteem and may lead to school aversion or even dropping out. Peer ostracism and teasing are especially common consequences for boys with the disorder.

Boys with gender identity disorder often show marked feminine mannerisms and speech patterns.

Many individuals with gender identity disorder become socially isolated.

The disturbance can be so pervasive that the mental lives of some individuals revolve only around activities that lessen gender distress. They are often preoccupied with appearance, especially early in the transition to living in the opposite sex role. Relationships with parents also may be seriously impaired. Some males with gender identity disorder resort to self-treatment with hormones and may (very rarely) perform their own castration or penectomy [surgical removal of the penis]. Especially in urban centers, some males with the disorder may engage in prostitution, placing them at a high risk for human immunodeficiency virus (HIV) infection. Suicide attempts and substance-related disorders are common.

Children with gender identity disorder may manifest coexisting separation anxiety disorder, generalized anxiety disorder and symptoms of depression.

Adolescents are particularly at risk for depression and suicidal ideation and suicide attempts.

Adults may display anxiety and depressive symptoms. Some adult males have a history of transvestic fetishism as well as other paraphilias [sexual deviations]. Associated personality disorders are more common among males than among females being evaluated at adult gender clinics.

Symptoms

Children:

- Express the desire to be the opposite sex

- Have disgust with their own genitals

- Believe that they will grow up to become the opposite sex

- Are rejected by their peer group and feel isolated

- Have depression

- Have anxiety

Adults:

- Desire to live as a person of the opposite sex

- Wish to be rid of their own genitals

- Dress in a way that is typical of the opposite sex

- Feel isolated

- Have anxiety

To be clinically diagnosed with GID:

A. Must persistently and strongly identify with the opposite gender (aside from desiring any perceived cultural advantage of being the other gender). . . .

In adolescents and adults, the disturbance is manifested by symptoms such as a stated desire to be the other sex, frequent passing as the other sex, desire to live or be treated as the other sex, or the conviction that he or she has the typical feelings and reactions of the other sex.

B. A persistent discomfort with his or her sex or sense of inappropriateness in the gender role of that sex. Must have strong discomfort with own gender and may express these qualities:

Boys:

- Disgust with own genitals

- Belief that genitals will disappear or that it would be preferable not to have a penis

- Rejection of male activities such as rough and tumble play, games and toys

Girls:

- Rejection of urinating in seated position

- Desire not to develop breasts or menstruate

- Claims that she will have a penis

- Strong dislike for typical female clothing

In adolescents and adults, the disturbance is manifested by symptoms such as preoccupation with getting rid of primary and secondary sex characteristics (such as request for hormones, surgery or other procedures to physically alter sexual characteristics to simulate the other sex) or belief that he or she was born the wrong sex.

C. The disturbance is not concurrent with physical intersex condition.

D. The disturbance causes clinically significant distress or impairment in social occupational or other important areas of functioning.

The cause is unknown, but hormonal influences in the womb, genetics and environmental factors (such as parenting) are suspected to be involved.

Causes

People with gender identity disorder act and present themselves as members of the opposite sex. The disorder may affect self-concept, choice of sexual partners and the display of femininity or masculinity through mannerisms, behavior and dress.

The feeling of being in the body of the "wrong" gender must persist for at least two years for this diagnosis to be made. The cause is unknown, but hormonal influences in the womb, genetics and environmental factors (such as parenting) are suspected to be involved. The disorder may occur in children or adults, and is rare.

There are no recent studies to provide data on prevalence of gender identity disorder. Data from some countries in Europe suggest that roughly 1 per 30,000 adult males and 1 per 100,000 adult females seek sex-reassignment surgery.

Onset of cross-gender interests and activities is usually between ages 2 and 4 years, and some parents report that their child has always had cross-gender interests. Only a very small number of children with gender identity disorder will continue to have symptoms that meet criteria for the disorder in later adolescence or adulthood. Typically, children are referred around the time of school entry because of parental concern that what they regarded as a phase does not appear to be passing.

Adult onset is typically in early to mid-adulthood, usually after or concurrent with transvestic fetishism. There are two different courses for the development of gender identity disorder:

- The first, typically found in late adolescence or adulthood, is a continuation of GID that had an onset in childhood or early adolescence.

- In the other course, the more overt signs of cross-gender identification appear later and more gradually, with a clinical presentation in early to mid-adulthood usually following, but sometimes concurrent with, transvestic fetishism.

The later-onset group:

- may be more fluctuating in the degree of cross-gender identification

- more ambivalent about sex-reassignment surgery

- more likely to be sexually attracted to women

- less likely to be satisfied after sex-reassignment surgery.

- Males with gender identity disorder who are sexually attracted to males tend to present in adolescence or early childhood with a lifelong history of gender dysphoria. In contrast, those who are sexually attracted to females, to both males and females or to neither sex tend to present later and typically have a history of transvestic fetishism. If gender identity disorder is present in adulthood, it tends to have a chronic course, but spontaneous remission has been reported.

Treatments

Individual and family counseling is recommended for children, and individual or couples therapy is recommended for adults. Sex reassignment through surgery and hormonal therapy is an option, but severe problems may persist after this form of treatment. A better outcome is associated with the early diagnosis and treatment of this disorder.

2

Transgender People Should Not Be Labeled with Mental Disorders

Kelley Winters

Kelley Winters, founder of the transgender activism group GID (Gender Identity Disorder) Reform Advocates, serves on the advisory board for the Matthew Shepard Foundation.

The psychological classification of gender identity disorder (GID) marginalizes and infringes on the civil rights of transgender people. GID reinforces negative and false stereotypes about adults and children who are gender variant, and the classification does not support the medical necessity of sex reassignment through surgery and treatment. Transgender people are not disordered; much of their emotional distress and at-risk behavior is caused by social intolerance and prejudice. Furthermore, it is illogical that a set of normal and expected behaviors of gender—mannerisms and dress—can be described as abnormal for one group of people and not others.

*T*he *Diagnostic and Statistical Manual of Mental Disorders (DSM)*, published by the American Psychiatric Association [APA], is regarded as the medical and social definition of mental disorder throughout North America and strongly influences the *The International Statistical Classification of Diseases and Related Health Problems (ICD)*. The diagnosis of Gender Identity Disorder (GID) in the Fourth Edition, Text

Kelley Winters, "Issues of GID Diagnosis for Transsexual Women and Men," GID Reform Advocates White Paper, 2010. Reproduced by permission.

Revision, of the *DSM* (*DSM-IV-TR*) has long raised concern among mental health professionals and civil rights advocates. There remains a need for some kind of diagnostic nomenclature to facilitate access to medically necessary hormonal and surgical transition care for transsexual individuals who need them. However, in its current form, the GID category is written to contradict rather than facilitate gender role and medical transition. The Gender Identity Disorder diagnosis in the *DSM-IV-TR* inflicts harm to gender variant, and especially transsexual, people in three ways: unfair social stigma, barriers to transition medical care for those who need it, and implicit promotion of gender-reparative psychiatric "treatment."

Unfair Social Stigma

The GID diagnosis labels gender identities and expressions which differ from expectations of assigned birth sex as mental illness and sexual deviance. The very name, Gender Identity Disorder, suggests that diagnosable gender identities are in themselves disordered, deficient, or illegitimate, representing perversion, delusion or immature development.

This message is reinforced in diagnostic criteria and supporting text that emphasize difference from cultural norms rather than actual distress with physical sex characteristics or assigned gender roles. Conflicting and ambiguous language conflates cultural nonconformity with mental illness and pathologize ordinary behaviors as symptomatic. The Introduction to the *DSM-IV-TR* states:

> Neither deviant behavior ... nor conflicts that are primarily between the individual and society are mental disorders unless the deviance or conflict is a symptom of dysfunction...

However, this principle is contradicted in the Gender Identity Disorder supporting text:

Gender Identity Disorder can be distinguished from simple nonconformity to stereotypical sex role behavior by the extent and pervasiveness of the cross-gender wishes, interests, and activities.

The second statement implies that one may deviate from social expectation without a label of mental illness, but not too much.

The current Gender Identity Disorder diagnosis actually poses barriers to access to medically necessary hormonal and surgical transition treatment for those who need them.

Thus, behavior and self expression that would be ordinary or even exemplary for all other women and men are mischaracterized in the GID diagnosis as symptomatic of madness. For example, shaving legs for adolescent transwomen and male identified men is described as symptomatic, even though it is common among males involved in certain athletics. Adopting ordinary behaviors, dress and mannerisms of the affirmed gender is described as a manifestation of preoccupation for adults who have transitioned in their social gender roles. It is not clear how these behaviors can be pathological for one group of people and not for another.

Across North America, the Gender Identity Disorder diagnosis is cited when gender variant adults and adolescents are denied human dignitiy, civil justice, and legal recognition in their affirmed gender roles. Gender variant and especially transsexual people lose jobs, homes, families, access to public facilities, and even custody and visitation of children as consequences of these false stereotypes.

Transition Medical Care Access

The transgender community and civil rights advocates have long been polarized by fear that access to medical transition procedures would be lost if the GID classification were revised. In truth, however, this is a false dilemma. The current Gender Identity Disorder diagnosis actually poses barriers to access to medically necessary hormonal and surgical transition treatment for those who need them.

The focus of medical treatment recommended by recognized Standards of Care, published by the World Professional Association for Transgender Health (WPATH), has long emphasized relieving distress with one's physical sex characteristics or assigned social gender role, termed gender dysphoria, and not on attempting to change one's gender identity. In fact, distress and impairment became central to the definition of mental disorder in the *DSM-IV* in 1994, when a generic clinical significance criterion was added to most diagnostic categories, including Gender Identity Disorder. However, while the scope of mental disorder was narrowed by the American Psychiatric Association, GID was broadened from the prior diagnosis of Transsexualism to include gender variant individuals who were not transsexual. The diagnostic criteria and supporting text were expanded to emphasize gender identity and expression nonconforming to assigned birth sex. The result was false-positive diagnosis of gender variant people who did not meet the APA definition of mental disorder and deemphasis of gender dysphoria for those who needed access to medical transition care.

The current Clinical Significance Criterion for GID requires clinically significant distress or impairment but is ambiguously written to conflate distress of gender dysphoria with distress caused by societal prejudice. Ego-syntonic subjects, satisfied with their current bodies and social roles with no need or further need for transition treatment, may remain diagnosable only because they are victims of discrimination. For example, the supporting text lists relationship difficulties and impaired function at work or school as examples of distress and disability with no reference to the role of societal intolerance as the cause. Sex work, HIV risk, suicide attempts and substance abuse are described as associated features of GID, when they are in truth consequences of discrimination and undeserved shame.

Gender-reparative, or Gender Identity Conversion therapies with a GID diagnosis have historically included torturous aversion therapies, psychotropic drugs and even institutionalization.

Tolerant, supportive, clinicians may infer that transgender identity or expression are not inherently impairing, just as sexual orientation is not inherently impairing for gay and lesbian people. Intolerant clinicians, on the other hand, are free to infer the opposite: that gender identities or expressions in themselves constitute impairment, regardless of the individual's happiness or well-being. Thus, the *DSM* does not acknowledge the existence of many healthy, happy post-transition transsexual or gender variant people or differentiate them from those who could benefit from medical treatment. In fact, there is no clear exit path from diagnosis for transitioned or post-operative transsexuals, however well adjusted. The supporting text lists post-surgical complications as "associated physical examination findings" of GID.

The diagnostic criteria, supporting text and categorical placement of GID contradict social and medical transition and mis-characterize transition itself as symptomatic of mental disorder. Transitioned individuals who are highly functional and happy with their lives forever remain diagnosable as mentally disordered, according to the diagnostic criteria in the *DSM-IV-TR*. As a consequence, the medical necessity of hormonal and surgical transition treatments are not commonly recognized by care providers, insurers and government agencies. In the US, only the financially privileged have access to surgical care, with few exceptions.

Gender-Reparative Psychotherapies

The Gender Identity Disorder diagnosis implicitly promotes cruel gender-reparative psychiatric "treatments" intended to enforce conformity to assigned birth sex and suppress gender variant identities and expressions into the closet. Once diagnosed with GID, the only way for a person to exit the current diagnostic criteria is to acquiesce to the assigned birth sex and completely hide his or her gender identity and deny his or her authentic self. Adults and adolescents, already at risk from undeserved shame and guilt, may be subjected to yet more shame and guilt at the hands of clinicians intolerant of gender diversity. Gender-reparative, or Gender Identity Conversion therapies with a GID diagnosis have historically included torturous aversion therapies, psychotropic drugs and even institutionalization.

Contempt for gender diversity and gender role transition is exemplified by maligning language throughout the diagnostic criteria and supporting text of the current GID diagnosis. Of the verbal degradation faced by gender variant people in North America, none is more damaging or hurtful than that which disregards their affirmed gender identities, denies the legitimacy of those who have transitioned and relegates them to their assigned birth sex. Throughout the diagnostic criteria and supporting text, the affirmed gender identities and social role for transsexual individuals is termed "other sex." In the supporting text, subjects are offensively labeled by birth sex and not their experienced affirmed gender. Transsexual women are repeatedly termed "males," and "he." For example,

> For some *males* . . . , the individual's sexual activity with a woman is accompanied by the fantasy of being lesbian lovers or that *his* partner is a man and he is a woman.

Thus, transwomen are consequently maligned as crazy and sexually suspect "men" by this language and vice versa for transmen. Most disturbing, the term "autogynephilia" was introduced in the supporting text of the *DSM-IV-TR* to demean lesbian transsexual women who are attracted to women:

> Adult *males* who are sexually attracted to females, . . . usually report a history of erotic arousal associated with the thought or image of oneself as a woman (termed *autogynephilia*).

The implication is that all lesbian transsexual women are incapable of attraction to their female partners but are instead possess a narcissistic sexual obsession with themselves.

Maligning pronouns and terms such as "autogynephilia" in the current GID diagnosis denote an intent by its authors to undermine the legitimacy of affirmed identities and social roles that differ from birth-assignment. Together with diagnostic criteria that describe nonconformity to assigned birth sex as mental disorder, they imply that suppressing these authentic identities and roles represents a favorable outcome.

The Fifth Edition of the *Diagnostic and Stastical Manual* (*DSM-5*), scheduled for 2013, represents an opportunity for the American Psychiatric Association to reform and redefine the Gender Identity Disorder diagnosis to simultaneously address issues of unfair social stigma, barriers to medical transition care, and promotion of cruel gender-reparative therapies. This might best be accomplished by replacing GID with nomenclature emphasizing painful distress with current physical sex characteristics or ascribed social gender role that are incongruent with inner gender identity, rather than nonconformity to assigned birth-sex.

3

The Transgender Rights Movement Is Necessary

Paisley Currah, Richard M. Juang, and Shannon Price Minter

Paisley Currah is an associate professor of political science at Brooklyn College. Richard M. Juang is an assistant professor of English at Susquehanna University. Shannon Price Minter is the legal director of the National Center for Lesbian Rights.

The movement for transgender rights has made significant advances during the past thirty years, leading to inclusion in nondiscrimination and hate crime laws in cities and states throughout the nation. However, in the majority of the United States, transgender people are nonpeople in the eyes of the law, with no rights to marry, use a public bathroom, or walk the streets in peace. Even getting their sex changed on birth certificates and driver's licenses is all but impossible. Discrimination against transgender people is essentially gender inequality, and individuals who do not conform to expected gender norms reserve the right to self-determination.

In the past thirty years, the transgender movement in the United States has gained surprising visibility and strength. In the legislative arena, transgender advocates have successfully fought for inclusion in nondiscrimination and hate crime laws in several states and dozens of municipalities. More than two hundred employers, including some Fortune 500 compa-

Paisley Currah, Richard M. Juang, and Shannon Price Minter, eds., "Introduction," *Transgender Rights*, Minneapolis, MN: University of Minnesota Press, 2006. Copyright © 2006 by the Regents of the University of Minnesota. All rights reserved. Reproduced by permission.

nies, and more than sixty colleges and universities now include gender identity in their nondiscrimination policies. In 2004, overturning decades of prior case law, a federal court of appeals ruled for the first time that transgender people who are discriminated against in the workplace are protected under Title VII of the Federal Civil Rights Act of 1964, which prohibits discrimination based on sex. Trans [transgender] activists have formed hundreds of social service and advocacy organizations, such as the Transgender Law Center in California, the Sylvia Rivera Law Project in New York, and the International Foundation for Gender Education. In several cities, trans activists have created community gender identity centers and clinics to counterbalance the power of doctors, therapists, and psychiatrists. Every major LGB [lesbian, gay, bisexual] national organization has changed its mission statement to include transgender people. In higher education, trans people are no longer simply an "object" of study in abnormal psychology textbooks. Rather, transgender issues have become a topic of serious and respectful inquiry in virtually every scholarly field, from medicine to political theory, and scholarly works by trans authors are now widely available.

At the same time, violence and discrimination against transgender people persists in daily life. In 2003 Gwen Araujo, a transgender teenager from a small town in Northern California, was murdered by a group of young men who beat her to death with a shovel after discovering that she had male genitalia. The attorneys representing the young men argued that their clients' actions were justified by Gwen's "deception" in not disclosing her transgender identity to them. Far from an isolated event, Gwen's brutal murder was one of thousands of similarly lethal hate crimes against transgender people that have been documented by the community Web site, Remembering Our Dead. While this epidemic of actual violence goes largely unnoticed by the mass media, it is an ever-present reality for transgender people—and especially for transgender women, who are most often the victims of such crimes. This vulnerability is amplified in prisons and jails, where transgender prisoners typically are housed by their birth sex and where transgender women are particularly vulnerable to rape by both fellow prisoners and guards.

Most transgender people still are deprived of any secure legal status.

The legal status of trans people in other arenas is equally precarious. In the past few years, appellate courts in Texas, Kansas, Ohio, and Florida have ruled that transsexual people are prohibited from marrying; in three of these cases, the courts held that marriages of many years' duration were null and void, simply because one of the spouses in each case was transsexual. In 2002 a federal court in Louisiana ruled that it was not discriminatory for Winn-Dixie to fire Peter Oiler for occasionally cross-dressing outside work. In prior decisions, federal courts routinely have excluded transsexual people from any protection under federal nondiscrimination laws, thereby leaving employers free to fire transsexual workers at will. In many states, obtaining a driver's license or birth certificate that reflects one's new gender is extremely difficult; in some, it is impossible.

In short, while the gains won by the U.S. transgender movement are impressive, most transgender people still are deprived of any secure legal status. In the eyes of the law in most states, they are nonpersons, with no right to marry, work, use a public bathroom, or even walk down the street in safety.

The Movement

What does transgender mean? Since about 1995, the meaning of *transgender* has begun to settle, and the term is now generally used to refer to individuals whose gender identity or expression does not conform to the social expectations for their assigned sex at birth. At the same time, related terms used to describe particular identities within that broader category have continued to evolve and multiply. As new generations of body modifiers and new social formations of gender resisters emerge, multiple usages coexist, sometimes easily, sometimes with much generational or philosophical tension: *transvestite, cross-dresser, trannie, trans, gender—, genderqueer, FTM, MtM, trans men, boyz, bois.* Transgender is an expansive and complicated social category.

The term *transgender* offers political possibilities as well as risks. Any claim to describe or define a people or a set of practices poses the danger of misrepresenting them. The danger is not trivial; distorted representations lead readily to misguided advocacy. The term can, at times, mask the differences among gender nonconforming people and risks implying a common identity that outweighs differences along racial and class lines. Nonetheless, there is also considerable value in a term that can draw together people who believe that individuals should have a right to determine and express their gender without fear, stigmatization, marginalization, or punishment.

One particular area of tension is the inclusion of intersex people in the definition of transgender. Intersex activists argue, rightly we think, that being intersex is not the same as being transgender. Being intersex denotes, according to [Northwestern University professor] Alice Dreger, "a variety of congenital conditions in which a person has neither the standard male nor the standard female anatomy." The attempt simply to assimilate intersex identities and political interests within a transgender rubric too often has meant ignoring the urgency of ending the surgical mutilation of intersex children. . . .

Ultimately, the effectiveness with which the transgender movement addresses the diversity of its constituents will depend less on finding a satisfactory vocabulary and more on how actual strategies for social change are implemented. The same is true for creating effective connections with people who do *not* see themselves as transgender. Put simply, the movement's effectiveness will depend heavily on who benefits from its successes.

Ultimately, *transgender* refers to a collective political identity. Whether we have psychological features in common or share a particular twist in our genetic codes is less important than the more pressing search for justice and equality.... It is a matter of fact that trans people conceive of themselves in many radically different ways: as transsexual women and men who have always known that they were female or male; as genderqueers living in an existential rebellion against the biopolitics of the dominant society; as butches who move complexly among lesbian and transgender identities and communities; as quietly androgynous femme boyz. Despite their profound differences, these groups all share a common political investment in a right to gender self-determination.

If it is wrong to fire someone for being a woman, it is equally wrong to fire someone for becoming a woman.

In practice, *transgender* is a useful term in many contexts, yet insufficiently inclusive or too imprecise in others. Many activists organize directly under the transgender rubric: the National Transgender Advocacy Coalition, the National Center for Transgender Equality, the Transgender Law and Policy Institute, and the Massachusetts Transgender Political Coalition. Other activists have embraced what appears to be a more universal term, *gender*: the International Foundation for Gender Education, Gender Education and Advocacy, the Gender Rights Advocacy Association of New Jersey, and Gender-PAC. Still other groups such as FTM International and American Boyz use more gender-specific labels to describe their constituencies. Nonetheless, when these groups seek justice and equality for people whose gender identity or expression contravenes social norms, they become facets of the same movement....

Law and Gender

Until recently, nondiscrimination laws did not define sex or gender. Consequently, it was left to the courts to decide whether discrimination against trans people should be recognized as a type of sex discrimination. The judiciary's record on this issue has been poor. The exemplary case in this area is *Ulane v. Eastern Airlines*, a 1984 case that is still binding precedent. In *Ulane*, a federal appellate court found that the plaintiff, a transsexual woman, was not discriminated against on the basis of sex. Rather, the court explained, "it is clear from the evidence that if Eastern did discriminate against Ulane, it was not because she is female, but because Ulane is a transsexual—a biological male who takes female hormones, cross-dresses, and has surgically altered parts of her body to make it appear to be female." The court's evasive logic has seemed weak even to people equipped with only a dictionary's definition of transsexuality; after all, it seems hardly an affront to reason to think that, if it is wrong to fire someone for being a woman, it is equally wrong to fire someone for becoming a woman. Nonetheless, this decision, and scores of others exactly like it, is symptomatic of the broader patterns of exclusion and misrepresentation faced by transgender people in the law.

Trans activists have put their energies into changing both laws and cultural perceptions. Perhaps the most visible strategy used to counter judicial hostility has been to ask legislatures to define sex, gender, or even sexual orientation within nondiscrimination laws so as to explicitly include trans people, or to add a new category, usually gender identity. At the same time, trans advocates have drawn on the tools provided by other civil rights movements to change the judiciary's understanding of who counts as a person deserving of protection. . . .

Foundations and Futures

If we return to foundational questions, perhaps the most important one to ask is, simply, "why rights?" For some, the rolling back of the gains of the traditional civil rights movement and the critique of identity-based movements as insufficiently inclusive and incapable of addressing nonidentitarian concerns such as class and poverty lead to a belief that activists and theorists must find a better focus of political practice. Nonetheless, rights discourse remains the commonsense of politics in the United States. The idea of rights provides a familiar, and thus quietly powerful, lexicon through which to challenge injustice. This is particularly the case when violence and exclusion are clearly targeted at particular *kinds* of persons.

Discrimination on the basis of gender nonconformity is, by its very nature, gender discrimination.

What needs to change? Protections on paper are, of course, inadequate. The legal recognition of trans people is meaningful only when it is part of a larger cultural transformation. For example, although Minnesota has included trans people in its nondiscrimination law since 1993, that state's highest court ruled in 2001 that Julie Goins had not been discriminated against when her employer told her she could not use the women's bathroom. The judges in that decision understood quite clearly that the law prohibited discrimination on the basis of "having or being perceived as having a self-image or identity not traditionally associated with one's biological maleness or femaleness." Nonetheless, it seemed nonsensical to them that Goins should have access to women-only space. The success of rights-based arguments depends on creating a culture in which trans people are not just a curiosity or a perversion of nature. At the same time, struggles organized around civil rights are also a form of cultural work. For example, including transgender people in hate crime laws does not create change by enhancing penalties but by educating legislators, the media, the police, and the courts about the violence faced by trans people and by asking the public at large to side with the victims rather than the perpetrators of hate.

Why *transgender* rights? Feminism already has established the ethical and legal basis for gender equality. The idea of gender equality includes transgender people, and so it may seem redundant to argue for the specific inclusion of transgender persons in nondiscrimination legislation. Logically, transgender people already should be covered by existing gender nondiscrimination laws; discrimination on the basis of gender nonconformity is, by its very nature, gender discrimination. In practice, however, courts, civil society, and the mass media typically have failed to apply the principle of gender equality to transgender people. One reason for this broad failure of logic and imagination is that trans people have been seen as examples of sexual "deviants," in the same way that homosexuals have been cast as gender inverts. As a consequence, the transgender movement, . . . has continued to be affiliated more strongly with the LGB movement than with the feminist movements that began in the 1960s and 1970s, despite significant conflicts. In the legal arena, the transgender rights movement has striven to expand the inclusivity of the term *gender* beyond its current cultural and legal boundaries; similarly, our political goals also have the potential to close the significant gaps created by the institutional separation between, LGB and women's rights advocacy.

The transgender movement is a highly accelerated and fragile reality. In thirty years, trans people have moved from meeting in secret to lobbying Congress, from being arrested for cross-dressing to mobilizing public protests against transphobic violence. . . . But in reaching our goals, transgender people will not disappear as a constituency or identity. Instead, transgender political work will take on different forms and become reoriented toward other projects and goals. Achieving equality will not be an end for trans people, but the start of a dramatic widening of the cultural and social imagination. What such a new world will look like, and what the transgender generations who live in it will make of their world, remains as yet unwritten.

4

The Transgender Rights Movement Is Harmful to Society

Traditional Values Coalition

Established in 1980, the Traditional Values Coalition is the largest nondenominational grassroots church lobby in the United States, representing the interests of more than 43,000 Christian churches to politicians and policy makers.

The transgender movement aims not only to normalize the behaviors of crossdressers, transvestites, and drag queens, but to give special legal protection to people engaging in these behaviors. Transgender activists also desire to deconstruct male and female identity and to push gender confusion onto children and parents and into the mainstream. But maleness and femaleness cannot be changed or created—these traits are tied to DNA. A man who undergoes hormone treatments and has his genitals removed does not alter his biological sex. Instead, he suffers from a mental disturbance that is the product of a troubled family life and requires psychiatric treatment.

Lesbian, Gay, Bisexual, and Transgender activists (LGBT) are working to add "sexual orientation," "gender," and "gender identity" to federal legislation. If this legislation is passed, cross-dressers, transsexuals, and drag queens will have federally protected minority status equal to minority groups.

Traditional Values Coalition, "A Gender Identity Disorder Goes Mainstream," accessed February 2010. Reproduced by permission.

What Is a Transgender?

The term Transgender is an umbrella term coined by transgender activists to describe the following individuals: heterosexual cross-dressers; homosexual transvestites or drag queens; and transsexuals (individuals undergoing so-called sex change operations) and she-males.

Some of these individuals live their lives as she-males with both female and male sexual characteristics. These are deeply troubled individuals who need professional help, not societal approval or affirmation.

A History Lesson: Gender Bill of Rights?

In Houston [Texas], in August, 1993, at a meeting of the Second International Conference on Transgender Law and Employment Policy, transgender activists passed the "International Gender Bill of Rights."

These are deeply troubled individuals who need professional help, not societal approval or affirmation.

Here is the text of the Gender Bill of Rights:

All human beings carry within themselves an ever-unfolding idea of who they are and what they are capable of achieving. The individual's sense of self is not determined by chromosomal sex, genitalia, assigned birth sex, or initial gender role. Thus the individual's identity and capabilities cannot be circumscribed by what society deems to be masculine or feminine behavior.

It is fundamental that individuals have the right to define, and to redefine as their lives unfold, their own gender identity, without regard to chromosomal sex, genitalia, assigned birth sex, or initial gender role.

The Right to Free Expression of Gender Identity—Given the right to define one's own gender identity, all human beings have the corresponding right to free expression of their self-defined gender identity.

The Right to Control and Change One's Own Body—All human beings have the right to control their bodies, which includes the right to change their bodies cosmetically, chemically, or surgically, so as to express a self-defined gender identity.

The Right to Competent Medical and Professional Care—Given the individual right to define one's gender identity, and the right to change one's own body as a means of expressing a self-defined gender identity, no individual should be denied access to competent medical or other professional care on the basis of chromosomal sex, genitalia, assigned birth sex, or initial gender role.

The Right to Freedom from Psychiatric Diagnosis or Treatment—Given the right to define one's own gender identity, individuals should not be subject to psychiatric diagnosis or treatment solely on the basis of their gender identity or role.

The Right to Sexual Expression—Given the right to a self-defined gender identity, every consenting adult has a corresponding right to free sexual expression.

The Right to Form Committed, Loving Relationships and Enter into Marital Contracts—Given that all human beings have the right to free expression of a self-defined gender identity, and the right to sexual expression as a form of gender expression, all human beings have a corresponding right to form committed, loving relationships with one another and to enter into marital contracts, regardless of either partner's chromosomal sex, genitalia, assigned birth sex, or initial gender role.

The Right to Conceive or Adopt Children; the Right to Nurture and Have Custody of Children and Exercise of Parental

Rights—Given the individual's right to form a committed, loving relationship with another, and to enter into marital contracts with another, together with the right to sexual expression of one's gender identity, all individuals have a corresponding right to conceive or adopt children, to nurture children and to have custody of children, and to exercise parental rights with respect to children, natural or adopted, without regard to chromosomal sex, genitalia, assigned birth sex, or initial gender role.

Transgenders Are Mentally Disordered

The American Psychiatric Association (APA) still lists Transsexualism and Transvestism as paraphilias or mental disorders in the *Diagnostic and Statistical Manual (DSM-IV-TR)*. However, homosexual groups such as the Human Rights Campaign (HRC) and GenderPac are pushing hard to have this classification removed from the *DSM*. The objective is to normalize a mental disorder in the same way that homosexuality was normalized in 1973 when psychiatrists removed this sexual dysfunction from the *DSM*. In fact, when the APA met in May, 2003 in San Francisco, Dr. Charles Moser with the Institute for Advanced Study of Human Sexuality, argued that sado-masochism, transsexualism/transvestism, and even bestiality (sex with animals) should be removed from the *DSM*. According to Moser, psychiatry no longer has a "base line" to judge what constitutes normal behavior, so these categories should be removed.

Media Is Aiding Transgender Movement

Hollywood and the liberal media are doing their part to normalize this serious mental illness. In 2001, for example, the *Los Angeles Times* published "Era of the Gender Crosser," that portrayed transgendered individuals as a misunderstood and persecuted minority. According to author Mary McNamara, individuals who believe they are the opposite sex should be treated as if they have a medical condition, not a mental condition.

The Discovery Health Channel repeatedly runs "What Sex Am I?" which questions the reality of male and female.

Hollywood is pushing the transgender agenda in various ways. HBO ran "Normal," in March, 2003. This show described a middle-aged married man who decided he was really a woman and sought a sex change. Networks are also running "Brandon Teena," about a poor sexually confused girl who dressed like a boy. She was eventually murdered by two angry young men when they discovered she she was. Teena Brandon has become a martyr for the transgender cause.

The latest martyr for transgender activists is a boy named Justin Zapata, who dressed like a girl and called himself "Angie."

Justin was brutally murdered in 2008 by a Mexican gang member who briefly "dated" Justin until he found out that "Angie" was actually an 18-year-old boy. The gang member has been sentenced to life in prison without parole—plus an extra sentence for committing a "hate crime" against Zapata.

Hollywood, which is dominated in many areas by homosexual activists, will continue to introduce transgender themes into its movies and TV shows.

The Transgender movement is also being helped by psychiatrists and pediatricians who are pushing the view that children should be free to choose their own "genders."

Transgender activists are also receiving help from journalists. The National Lesbian and Gay Journalists Association, for example, has distributed to media outlets a "Stylebook Supplement." It encourages journalists to cater to the transgender agenda by referring to transgendered persons by their self-identification, not their actual birth sex.

Psychiatrists and Pediatricians Are Pushing Transgender Confusion on Kids

The Transgender movement is also being helped by psychiatrists and pediatricians who are pushing the view that children should be free to choose their own "genders."

In May, 2006, the Pediatric Academic Societies held a conference in San Francisco to promote this bizarre viewpoint.

A member of the National Association for Research and Therapy of Homosexuality (NARTH) was an eyewitness at this conference and described what occurred at this conference.

Two of the attendees were Irene N. Sills and Arlene Istar Lev. They presented a paper titled, "Gender-Variant Youth— The Role of the Pediatrician." They outlined a "non-pathological model for transgender expression" designed to "help identify the gender-variant child as one who simply marches to the beat of a different drummer."

Pro-transgender activists like these are referring to children with serious Gender Identity Disorders as merely "gender variant."

Some pro-transgender pediatricians are actually injecting pre-teens with hormones to keep them from developing into adult males or females—until these kids "decide" what sex they wish to be.

This is child abuse, yet the transgender agenda is well-advanced in academia and in the medical and mental health professions.

No One Can Change Their Sex

The reality is that no person can actually change into a different sex. Maleness and femaleness are in the DNA and are unchangeable. A man who has his sex organ removed and takes hormone treatments to grow female breasts is still genetically a male. He is simply a mutilated man, not a woman. This fiction, however, is being perpetrated by a perverted sexual ideology—not by biological facts or science.

Homosexual groups such as the Human Rights Campaign and the National Gay and Lesbian Task Force have provided transgender activists with credibility and political power as they pursue their agenda.

The transgender movement's philosophy is based upon the writings of several transsexuals. Among them are Nancy Nangeroni, founder of the International Foundation for Gender Education, Martine Rothblatt, and Marxist radical Leslie Feinberg, author of *Transgender Warrior*, and an editor with the Workers World Party, a Communist splinter group that aligns itself with North Korea.

Homosexuals and their transgender allies believe that "gender" is a cultural invention, not a biological reality.

Nancy Nangeroni claims that Western Civilization is "sick" because it pathologizes any person who wants a sex change operation. Martine Rothblatt is author of *The Apartheid of Sex: A Manifesto on the Freedom of Gender*. According to Rothblatt, our culture's practice of dividing people into two sexes is as evil as racial apartheid. He argues that there are actually several sexes, not just male and female. Those who oppose transgenderism are "transphobic" and intolerant.

The Human Rights Campaign, one of the most aggressive homosexual groups in the United States, is allied with transgender activists and has actually developed workplace guidelines for how businesses should handle men and women who are undergoing sex change operations.

In addition, Parents and Friends of Lesbians and Gays (PFLAG) has a special Transgender Special Outreach Network, which includes coordinators in more than 170 chapters. It also distributed 12,000 copies of "Our Trans Children" to schools and to parents of these sexually confused children.

The leading transgender group is GenderPac, headed by male-to-female transgender Riki Wilchins. He is author of *READ MY LIPS: Sexual Subversion & The End of Gender*. Wilchins works closely with the NGLTF [National Gay and Lesbian Task Force] to get the American Psychiatric Association to remove Transsexualism as a mental disorder. Patricia Ireland, former head of the YWCA, is a member of the board of GenderPac and helps lobby Congress for passage of legislation protecting the "gender identity" of individuals in the workplace and in our culture.

One cannot change into a different sex.

Be Whatever You Wish

Homosexuals and their transgender allies believe that "gender" is a cultural invention, not a biological reality. According to these activists, a person can self-identify and be whatever he or she wishes to be sexually. One pro-transgender activist, Professor Anne Fausto-Sterling, for example, has said that "Complete maleness and complete femaleness represent the extreme ends of a spectrum of possible body types."

Fausto-Sterling published "The Five Sexes: Why Male and Female Are Not Enough," in *The Sciences*, March/April 1993. In fact, many of these sexually confused individuals decide that they wish to be either male nor female, but to exist as she-males with female sexual characteristics from the waist up and male sexual characteristics from the waist down.

One of these individuals actually set up a web site to describe herself. Della Grace on her web site "Body Politic," says she is a she-male and former lesbian photographer and visual artist. Grace says she willingly purchased a "one-way ticket" to "no man's land," to inhabit the "nether world" where she is neither male nor female. She calls herself a "pansexual, which means I don't discriminate on the basis of gender or species." She also describes herself as a "gender variant" mutant who has decided against being male or female.

Deconstructing Male and Female

The National Association for Research and Therapy of Homosexuality (NARTH) has published numerous articles on various Gender Identity Disorders. One is by Dale O'Leary, author of *The Gender Agenda*. In the NARTH paper, "Destabilizing The Categories Of Sex And Gender," O'Leary notes: Patients who suffer from the belief that they are men trapped in the bodies of women (or women trapped in the bodies of men) need real help. . . . The promotion of 'sex changes,' and the normalizing of severe gender identity disorders by radical feminists, pro-same-sex attraction disorder activists, and sexual revolutionaries is part of their larger agenda—namely the destabilization of the categories of sex and gender."

O'Leary notes that radicals and medical professionals who promote sex change operations are operating under the delusion that one's gender is changeable. One cannot change into a different sex. It is genetically and medically impossible. Gender confused individuals need long-term counseling, not approval for what is clearly a mental disturbance.

Dr. Martin Silverman, a member of NARTH, has written extensively on Gender Identity Disorders. In a NARTH paper, "Gender Identity Disorder In Boys: A Complemental Series?" he notes that a boy who has developed a Gender Identity Disorder such as homosexuality or transvestism, typically comes from a home where the mother is smothering in her love and where the father is passive and feels powerless to overcome his wife's dominance in the family. . . .

What Can Be Done?

If the transgender movement is not already active in your community, it will be. Wherever there are homosexual activist groups, you will find transgendered individuals working along-side them to establish policies and recruitment programs in public schools and to change laws to redefine what it means to be male or female. Here are some suggestions for action:

Monitor city and state legislative proposals that contain the word "gender" in them. Gender is code for cross-dressers, transvestites, and transsexuals. Inform your local politicians of this cultural agenda so they will recognize it when activists attempt to push through legislation.

Oppose Gay Straight Alliance clubs on school campuses. These are recruitment programs to lure children into sexually destructive lifestyles.

These GLSEN [Gay, Lesbian and Straight Education Network]-sponsored groups are now promoting cross-dressing for children.

Use TVC [Traditional Values Coalition], NARTH and other materials in fighting homosexual/transgenderism.

5

Christians Should Be Compassionate Toward Transgender People

John W. Kennedy

John W. Kennedy is a consulting editor at Christianity Today *and a journalist based in Springfield, Missouri.*

The transgender rights movement is becoming more visible in the mainstream public. Within the church, Christians should show compassion and not shun transgender people. In fact, evangelical churches are unprepared to face the challenge of welcoming people suffering from gender identity disorder (GID) and balancing the teachings of church doctrine on sexuality and creation. Still, pastors and church members must reinforce to these individuals in need that transgender behavior conflicts with the Bible, and God does not make mistakes in gender. Faith, church-based care, and psychiatric counseling can help transgender people overcome struggles of sexual identity and confusion.

John Nemecek struggled with gender confusion from early childhood. Marrying at age 21 didn't change that confusion. Neither did raising three sons—all of whom are themselves now happily married. Four years ago, Nemecek's Internet search of a medical site matched the symptoms he exhibited: gender identity disorder (GID). "It was an awesome experience to realize something I'd been dealing with all my life had a name," Nemecek says. A therapist, endocrinologist, and a counselor all later confirmed the diagnosis.

John W. Kennedy, "The Transgender Moment," *Christianity Today*, February 2008. Reproduced by permission of the author.

In 2004, Nemecek began taking female hormones, a process that will last his lifetime. However, there will be no sex reassignment surgery. Nemecek is staying with his wife, Joanne, and they recently celebrated 35 years of marriage.

Nemecek, 56, may now feel he has more clarity about gender identity, but much ambiguity remains. Nemecek's driver's license says "male," but on credit card applications, Nemecek writes "female." Since John and Joanne wed legally, their marriage isn't illegal, even though it appears they are in a lesbian union.

In 2005, Nemecek's employer, Spring Arbor University, learned of John's plans for a court-approved change of first name to "Julie." Afterwards, the Free Methodist-affiliated school in southern Michigan cut Nemecek's pay and reduced [his] job responsibilities. Eventually, Spring Arbor decided not to rehire the business professor and associate dean when Nemecek started wearing a wig, makeup, fingernail polish, and earrings on campus. Nemecek was a 15-year veteran at the university, located in the small town of Spring Arbor, a conservative, churchgoing community of 2,100 people.

After the university's action, Nemecek filed an employment discrimination complaint with the Equal Employment Opportunity Commission, triggering newspaper headlines across the nation. (Federal courts have yet to settle completely whether federal protections against sexual discrimination in the workplace—Title VII of the Civil Rights Act—protect transgendered people. Several cases are working their way through the justice system.)

In March 2007, Spring Arbor decided to settle out of court, resolving the case and permanently ending Nemecek's employment there. At an official mediation hearing, the professor asked aloud, "Should I deny my head, heart, and soul to live according to what others think of my body? I cannot do that and live a life of Christian integrity."

Nemecek, who spent two decades as a Baptist pastor before joining Spring Arbor's faculty, is currently working as an independent consultant on gay, lesbian, bisexual, and transgender (GLBT) issues.

"This is something that's in you from the womb," says Nemecek.

Nemecek's transgender experience is still statistically rare, but the profile of transgender issues is rising, both in and outside the church, and evangelical churches and mental health professionals are beginning to respond.

Expanding Civil Rights

The drive to expand civil rights to include transgendered people is gaining momentum. Many films, magazine articles, TV programs, and newspaper commentaries trumpet this campaign, sympathizing with people who feel they have been unfairly targeted because of their transgender condition.

Such media portrayals, including several focusing on elementary-age children with supportive parents, typically blend a sense of injustice and pathos to convince viewers how wrong society has been to label transgendered people as deviant, strange, or sinful.

Advocates say transgendered individuals are at great risk of hate crimes and discrimination in housing and employment searches. In many jurisdictions, it's legal for an employer to dismiss or refuse to hire an individual for being transgendered. A website, *gender.org*, lists the names of transgendered murder victims. To increase public awareness, advocates have chosen November 20 as the annual National Transgender Day of Remembrance for transgendered victims from the past year.

There is little research on the public's opinion of transgender behavior. One 2002 poll for the Human Rights Campaign found that 48 percent of the people surveyed would have "no problem working with a transgendered person."

Experts believe there are about 400,000 transgendered persons, less than one-half of one percent of the population, in America. In order to be diagnosed with gender identity disorder, there must be a strong desire to be the other sex and a persistent discomfort with one's body. The person may or may not have had sex reassignment surgery, and he or she may or may not have homosexual attractions.

There are six levels of GID according to what is known as the Harry Benjamin Scale. The occasional cross-dresser is stage one; someone who has had a surgical procedure, such as a vaginectomy or penectomy [surgical removal of the vagina or penis], has completed the final step.

A raft of transgender rights groups have formed in recent years to take up the civil rights cause. For example, there's the Transgender Legal Defense & Education Fund, the National Center for Transgender Equality, and the Transgender Law and Policy Institute. That's not to mention many sexual rights groups lending support. (The acronym GLBT is now a standard classification for such groups, referring to gays, lesbians, bisexuals, and transgendered persons.)

Intense activism for transgender inclusion is having a ripple effect on local churches.

Such groups are seeking more than additional restrooms. The most vocal campaign is for special federal protections for employment and housing. However, through multiple lawsuits, transgender rights organizations are defending the transgendered homeless, college students, immigrants, and prisoners.

As of January 2008, some 13 states have laws prohibiting employers and landlords from discriminating against transgendered people. Ten states have enacted hate crime laws explicitly protecting "gender identity or expression." A growing number of major corporations have gender identity nondiscrimination policies.

Intense activism for transgender inclusion is having a ripple effect on local churches. Pastors are more likely to encounter a GLBT activist than a church member with GID; few pastors are trained to address either transgender advocacy or those with GID.

Debating Sexual Ethics

When church leaders include a transgendered individual who has "come out" into the spiritual life and leadership of a local congregation, it almost always provokes sharp controversy. But a number of liberal religious groups are rallying around the transgender movement in the name of social justice. The Raleigh, North Carolina-based Faith in America is at the forefront.

"Religion has been used in history to discriminate against various groups of people by justifying slavery, denying women the right to vote, and persecuting religious minorities," says Jimmy Creech, executive director of Faith in America. "Today it is being used to persecute lesbian, gay, bisexual, and transgendered people."

The transgender movement clashes with traditional Christian theology that teaches the only God-given expression of human sexuality is between a man and woman who are married.

Creech likens the struggle for transgender liberties to the early civil rights movement to end racial bigotry. Creech, a former United Methodist Church (UMC) minister, says he spent three years studying Scripture before concluding that church teachings on homosexuality are fear-based and motivated by hate. Creech views the transgender movement as indistinguishable from the gay rights cause.

"We have to recognize the Bible in terms of the history and culture in which it was written," Creech says. "Scripture doesn't address the issues of transgender experience."

Whether mentioned in Scripture or not, the transgender movement clashes with traditional Christian theology that teaches the only God-given expression of human sexuality is between a man and woman who are married. "Transgender impulses are strong, but they don't match up with the Christian sexual ethic," says Warren Throckmorton, associate professor of psychology at Grove City College in Pennsylvania. "Desires must be brought into alignment with biblical teachings, but it will be inconvenient and distressful."

Throckmorton, past president of the American Mental Health Counselors Association, says he has advised transgendered people who are in absolute agony over their state. Typically, such individuals are desperately in search of hope and acceptance, he says. It may be uncomfortable to tell transgendered individuals that their desires don't align with the Bible, Throckmorton says, but pastors must do so. "Even if science does determine differentiation in the brain at birth," Throckmorton says, "even if there are prenatal influences, we can't set aside teachings of the Bible because of research findings."

As with homosexuality, it can be a delicate balance— accepting the person into the church without affirming that switching sexual identities is God's will for their lives.

So far, the church's response to transgender rights has been focused more on specific cases before denominational bodies or the civil courts, and less on the campaign for transgendered persons' rights. Those opposing the transgender movement are reluctant to call themselves experts because much about the condition remains a mystery and public debate is so new.

Individual evangelical congregations across the land are trying to figure out how to welcome lonely, hurting, seeking visitors who exhibit GID without offending long-term members.

As with homosexuality, it can be a delicate balance—accepting the person into the church without affirming that switching sexual identities is God's will for their lives.

A few years back, Calvary Assembly of God in Orlando, Florida, accepted a man who had complete sex reassignment surgery, and even allowed the person to do volunteer maintenance work at the church, according to administrator Bill Gray. The individual agreed to use a gender-neutral restroom in the office rather than upset females in the women's restroom.

One day, the individual appeared in Gray's office, weeping and confused. The person told Gray that after extensive counsel, he eventually realized that God didn't make creative mistakes and he resumed a male identity.

The everyday lives of transgendered people are often an agonizing interplay of nature and nurture.

Pushing the Envelope

In Congress, legislators during 2007 considered three bills addressing GLBT issues: The Matthew Shepard Act places sexual orientation and gender identity as new categories covered under the federal hate crimes law; the Employment Non-Discrimination Act provides employment protection for GLBT workers; and the Military Enhancement Readiness Act repeals the ban on GLBT participation in the military.

But in the short term, none of the bills, caught up in Washington politics, are expected to pass.

In Washington, vocal conservative organizations don't see transgender rights as a matter of civil liberties. "The transgender lobby is following the example of the homosexual lobby in that they are co-opting the language of the civil rights movement in order to push their own radical and wacky agenda," says Matt Barber, policy director for cultural issues for Concerned Women for America (CWA).

Barber points out that the American Psychiatric Association, which declassified homosexuality as a mental disorder in 1973, still classifies the condition of transgender as a disorder. Barber says the political left wing is facilitating more gender confusion by counseling the afflicted to feel good about themselves rather than find a treatment for this disorder. "You are what you are—male or female," Barber says.

Peter Sprigg, Family Research Council (FRC) vice president for policy in Washington, D.C., says, "The pressure for acceptance is ultimately a challenge to the authority of Scripture and a violation of natural law. In the gay, lesbian, bisexual, transgender movement there is a tendency to continually push the envelope in trying to demand the acceptance of what most people perceive to be unusual behavior."

The everyday lives of transgendered people are often an agonizing interplay of nature and nurture. The experience of Ann Gordon/Drew Phoenix has become a public example of this interplay in a faith-based environment.

As a child, Ann Gordon's parents allowed her to dress and act like a boy. Because of Ann's tomboyish appearance and conduct, her parents even publicly referred to her as their son in a small town north of Dayton, Ohio. But when puberty hit, Ann's parents expected her to start wearing dresses and look like a lady. She didn't know how to conform to parental wishes and societal expectations.

Eighteen years ago, Ann became an ordained United Methodist minister. In 2002, Ann began serving St. John's of Baltimore United Methodist Church (UMC). But the lifelong feelings of gender confusion were strong and persistent.

"I experienced a disconnect between my external physical self and my internal spiritual self," the minister says.

In 2006, Ann Gordon legally became Drew Phoenix, culminating in a sex-change operation. After the surgery, the bishop of the Baltimore-Washington conference reappointed

Phoenix to the church. Some 20 of the 40 active St. John's members view themselves as part of the GLBT movement, according to Phoenix.

"I have no qualms about the transition," says Phoenix, 48. "It was the right thing to do. I feel happy, peaceful, and whole. I felt guided by the Spirit to do this."

In October, the nine-member UMC Judicial Council met to determine if Phoenix had broken any church law. Nothing in the denomination's Book of Discipline addresses the topic. The council upheld the bishop's decision that Phoenix could remain as a pastor in good standing. This summer, the UMC General Conference, which meets every four years, will likely discuss banning transgendered ministers.

Phoenix sets aside the biological fact that her body was originally female. "I believe I was born male," Phoenix says. "My body didn't match what I am. That's how God made me. God created me male."

Alan Chambers, president of Exodus International in Orlando, Florida, understands the ordeal that Phoenix is facing. "As a prepubescent boy I could have been diagnosed as transgender," Chambers says. "I dressed like a girl. I acted like a girl. I wanted to be a girl." Chambers is convinced that many of the children labeled as transgendered have been misdiagnosed.

Chambers, 35, says his parents didn't encourage him to try to be a female. He says his parents knew God didn't make mistakes and cited Genesis 1:27, in which God creates male and female. Preschoolers are incapable of knowing whether they would feel better as the other gender, Chambers says. His desire to be a girl subsided when he hit puberty.

"A lot of parents are allowing their children to switch identities from the sex that God created them to live," Chambers says. "That only sets kids up to be even more confused."

Call for Compassion

Jerry Leach, director of Reality Resources, a ministry in Lexington, Kentucky, to people dealing with gender confusion, shares Chambers's point of view. Leach says, "Rather than cutting tissue by invasive surgery and starting a new life, which for the most part doesn't work, people need to find help psychiatrically."

Leach has become the referral point person for several national Christian organizations on this topic. "The essence of who you are in your genetics, anatomy, chromosomes, and DNA does not suddenly change by surgical amputation."

Surgery or no surgery, there is no quick fix for transgendered people. Chambers says those who wrestle with such feelings don't start out with a desire to be involved in sinful behavior. It's merely a response to what they feel is natural.

"It's a psychological, emotional struggle that needs compassion," Chambers says. "It's an identity issue. At its core, there is absolute confusion about who someone is created to be."

Leach says, "This is a psychological and emotional malady. It's not like taking an appendix out."

Leach, 65, says only the sympathy of trusted Christian friends helped him emerge from his own conflict.

Sexual identity struggles consumed Leach beginning in early boyhood. His parents told him they wished he had been a girl and that they had planned to name him Jennifer. His mother made him wear dresses. His father told him he looked better as a female. The pattern of cross-dressing, applying lipstick and mascara, and wearing fingernail polish and pantyhose became a secret obsession years into his adult life. While some men who gazed at scantily clad females were overcome with lust, Leach had a different problem: jealousy. He wished he inhabited those bodies himself.

With God's help, Leach has learned to avoid occasions of temptation, including shopping for dresses with Charlene, his wife of 46 years.

There is no human condition outside the redemptive circle of God's love and power.

Leach hoped marriage would make his gender-confused feelings go away, but it didn't. In 1989, after taking female hormones for 18 months, Leach scheduled sex reassignment surgery. But two weeks before the operation, he says he sensed God telling him to stop his covert double life.

Ultimately, Leach understood that God knit together his male body, as outlined in Psalm 139:15–16.

"God planned for me to be a man before I had ever been created," Leach says. "There was not a woman inside my body longing to be expressed. There is no human condition outside the redemptive circle of God's love and power."

The challenge before conservative evangelicals is persuading transgendered people, their families, and faith-based advocates that gender identity disorder is not beyond the reach of God's grace, compassionate church-based care, and professional help.

6

Transgender People Need Federal Protections in the Workplace

Meghan Stabler

Meghan Stabler is the principal strategic marketing manager at BMC Software in Houston, Texas.

Transgender people face widespread discrimination in the workplace, placing their finances and well-being in jeopardy. In thirty-eight states, people who come out as transgender or transsexual can be fired and have no laws protecting them. Many of these individuals have been terminated or demoted from their jobs on disclosure of their transition from their sex at birth despite their qualifications, merit, and professional experience. Such discrimination impacts access to health care, which is essential to those seeking sex-reassignment surgery and hormone treatment, and puts transgender people at higher risk of unemployment and homelessness.

Thank you for this opportunity to submit written testimony on the issue of gender identity and discrimination in the workplace. I commend the Subcommittee [of the U.S. House of Representatives] for holding the first hearing on this important topic. My statement will focus on the discrimination faced by so many transgender men and women in the

Meghan Stabler, "Prepared Written Statement of Meghan Stabler to the Subcommittee on Health, Employment, Labor, and Pensions, Committee on Education and Labor, U.S. House of Representatives: An Examination of Discrimination Against Transgender Americans in the Workplace," hrc.org, June 26, 2008. Reproduced by permission. Link to Senate testimony: http://www.hrcbackstory.org/wp-content/uploads/2009/11/Meghan-Stabler-Testimony-Senate-ENDA-Hearing-11.05.09.pdf workplace, and its implications on personal finances, health care and insurance availability. My testimony, and that of others, is given in the hopes that we enable inclusive workplace legislation to protect and not to discriminate against trans-workers.

My name is Meghan Stabler and first and foremost I am a software business executive, having worked for major corporations in Europe and in North America for the last 27 years. Before transitioning I enjoyed an amazing career with increasing responsibilities and an unlimited career path. I was married and have a wonderful daughter who just turned 15 this past weekend. Second, I am transgender, and a transsexual, meaning I transitioned genders, in my case from male to female (sometimes referred to as "MTF" or "transwoman"). Simply because I am transgender, employers are able to "fire" me in 38 states; simply because I am transgender, health care providers can deny me coverage.

Discrimination in the Workplace

My ability to finance health care coverage, and to provide myself with a home, is clearly linked to my ability to work and remain employed. Many transgender people face discrimination in the workplace, sometimes with employers terminating their jobs within hours of their coming out as transgender. Losing a job impacts access to health care, and faced with dwindling finances, can ultimately lead transgender people to homelessness. In 2006, the Transgender Law Center conducted a survey of transgender people living in San Francisco which found the following: only 25% of the transgender people surveyed were employed full time, and altogether 35% were unemployed. Only 4% made more than the estimated median income for San Francisco. A remarkable statistic, considering that the wider Bay Area is considered "home" to my profession of software, and even more remarkable as San Francisco is considered one of the most progressive cities in North America.

I, too, have experienced discrimination during, and following, my transition from male to female. Let me share my story first. Since my earliest memories I felt different, I did not feel right about my gender. This is known medically as Gender Identity Disorder. Simply put, my emotional and psychological gender was not in alignment with my genetic, physiological sex. This is not an acquired condition; rather, it is an intrinsic part, a lifelong aspect, of my being. Despite all of the behaviors that I learned in trying to deny my true feelings, this condition had been the source of unease and discomfort in my life. I received treatment through accepted medical practices for Gender Identity Disorder. While the types of medical or other treatment, if any, range widely, I took the necessary steps to change my physical gender from male to female. Doing so did not change the person I was or that I am, but finally dealing with this lifted a huge weight off my shoulders.

Without the income we may not have access to essential medications and treatments, or even expensive surgeries that enable us to slip back in to society in the new "legal" gender.

As a male in the workplace I enjoyed what I call "entitlements", I enjoyed a successful career, in meetings I was seen as a leader and I had employment protections. As I began to transition it changed. Initially there was no policy of protection in my place of work, but over time my employer was willing to place EEO [Equal Employment Opportunity] and Sexual Harassment policies in place. As a female in the workplace I see the "other side" of the business table, yet with a societal stigmatism labeled upon me as transgender, and like the majority of transgender persons I know, I have faced workplace issues.

Since I openly transitioned, I have received a number of job demotions: I am no longer a senior executive. As a result, I have seen significant salary reductions, along with reductions in my participation and involvement in meetings and business decisions. As a result, I face a monthly struggle to keep my house payments and related bills, whilst ensuring that I pay court-ordered child support. I have had to use much of my savings to make up shortfalls and bill payments, including my daughter's educational needs.

Not So Lucky

Having a job is so important to transgender people, without the income we may not have access to essential medications and treatments, or even expensive surgeries that enable us to slip back in to society in the new "legal" gender. Overall, I have been one of the lucky ones, yet I would like to cite a number of examples from friends that have not been so lucky.

First is the story of a transgender friend who transitioned over 5 years ago. She was a Chief Technology Officer in a software development company, but upon announcing her need to transition from male to female, she was terminated from her position. She faced immediate workplace discrimination. She relocated in the hopes that she could start a new life, without her male history following her. Over the coming months, and then years, her life savings dwindled to nothing despite her applying for jobs not only within her home state, but across the country and world. She was overlooked for many positions, and for those for which she received an initial call back, she never received a second. She used her remaining savings to complete some surgeries, as she still needed to resolve her inner need to change gender. With escalating costs and a declining source of finances, she became increasingly suicidal. Without a job and income, completing surgery was out of reach. She was very qualified for positions; her knowledge of technology never changed between the day she announced transition and the day prior to transition, yet she was never hired for a job for over five years.

Second is the experience of another good friend of mine, a commercial pilot, who was placed on paid-administrative leave within two hours of talking to her company's HR executives about her intent to transition genders. Within four days, the company asked her to tender her resignation. Almost a year after being fired, she was ready to fly again, but her FAA medical certificate had lapsed. Getting that certificate reinstated has taken nearly another year. In the past, renewing that certificate had taken her only hours, like renewing a driver's license. This is directly related to her Transgender status. Thankfully, a few weeks ago, and after completing many FAA mandated tests, she received her certificate to fly.

Third is the story of another friend, who was once a manufacturing engineer in a predominantly-male business. On announcing her need to transition, she was immediately terminated. She needed to complete transition, yet her finances were reduced and she found it increasingly hard to get a job in the line of work in which she was experienced. She relocated, but still could not find a position equal to her former job. After two years, despite her engineering expertise, she was working as a housekeeper in a Denver hotel.

I assure you that during any business day you have flown with, sat next to, ordered from, or talked to a transgender person.

An Essential Need

In conclusion, for transgender people, gender transition is not a choice, but is rather an essential need. Like the witnesses before you today, I have been and am still a productive, responsible, dedicated and passionate employee. It is only when we are subject to discriminatory actions and a lack of workplace protections that our work begins to suffer. Without work, we lose income. Without income or savings, we lack access to affordable healthcare, and sometimes healthcare is not even available to us from certain providers just because of our transitional history or status. Without healthcare we often cannot complete transition. With the stress placed on us, often suicide is a considered option.

As you have seen from the witnesses called before you today, we have varying careers, although some no longer are able to work in their chosen profession, if at all. Standing behind us in the fabric of America there are tens of thousands more who face continuing discrimination. Their voices cannot be here today, but I assure you that during any business day you have flown with, sat next to, ordered from, or talked to a transgender person.

In closing, I thank the subcommittee for listening to our perspective on the issue of gender identity and workplace discrimination and for its invitation to submit written testimony. I would like to leave you with this quote from Robert Francis Kennedy: "Each time a man stands for an ideal, or acts to improve the lot of others, or strikes out against injustice, he sends a tiny ripple of hope, and crossing each other from a million different centers of energy and daring, those ripples build a current which can sweep down the mightiest walls of oppression and resistance."

Once again, I thank you for allowing me to submit written testimony, and I hope that we can begin to remove workplace injustice and discrimination that so many transgender people face.

7

Transgender People Do Not Need Federal Protections in the Workplace

Glen Lavy

Glen Lavy is senior counsel at the Alliance Defense Fund, a Christian nonprofit organization in Scottsdale, Arizona.

Protecting transgender people and so-called expressions of gender with federal laws would trample on the religious and privacy rights of Americans. If enacted, faith-based organizations, centers, and businesses would be forced to hire or continue to employ workers who crossdress or identify themselves as genders contrary to their biological sex. Furthermore, transgender activists' definition of gender identity and expression is vague; it would create a dilemma for employers to discern an employee's "true" gender and open special protections to apply to virtually everyone. Women and girls also would have their privacy violated if transgender and transsexual men with male organs are allowed to use women's restrooms.

I am senior counsel at the Alliance Defense Fund [ADF]. For more than 7 years my colleagues and I at ADF have been working to protect the unique status of marriage as being between one man and one woman. Three times I have argued in support of marriage in the California courts, most recently in the California Supreme Court, and have been involved in

Glen Lavy, "Testimony of Glen Lavy to the Subcommittee on Health, Employment, Labor, and Pensions, Committee on Education and Labor, U.S. House of Representatives: An Examination of Discrimination Against Transgender Americans in the Workplace," Traditional Values Coalition, June 26, 2008. Reproduced by permission of the author.

some capacity in every major marriage case in the country. But the radical efforts to eliminate the unique, opposite-sex nature of marriage are only a precursor to the opposition's most dangerous principle. That principle is simply stated: that biological sex and gender are utterly divorced from one another. If the proponents of the idea that individuals have the right to pick their own gender succeed, upholding the definition of marriage as [between] a man and a woman will be meaningless.

Today I speak out of my experience because of the palpable danger to religious liberty and freedom of conscience if Congress were to define gender identity and expression as a protected class. Certainly there are individuals who suffer very real emotional strife from sexual confusion—it is a distinct psychological diagnosis in some cases. Declining to accommodate an employee's belief that he or she is actually a member of the opposite sex, however, is not a form of insidious discrimination. This is not an issue that should be the subject of federal legislation.

Religious Liberty and Rights of Conscience in the Workplace

It is important to recognize that religious objections to the concept of "transgender" are based on theological beliefs rather than discomfort with or fear of the unfamiliar. The concepts of male and female being established at birth and the two sexes being joined in marriage are integrally related to theological beliefs about the relationship between God and the church. Forcing persons with such beliefs to treat "transgender" as a valid concept is like forcing an Orthodox Jew to eat pork. Regardless of one's views of the merits of such beliefs, it is undeniable that such good faith beliefs exist. Trampling those beliefs raises serious constitutional issues under the First Amendment.

The sincerity of religious beliefs about male and female is why creating federal protection for gender identity and expression would have an unavoidable negative impact on religious liberty and rights of conscience in the workplace (providing such legislation were not ultimately deemed unconstitutional as applied to religious persons or organizations). The legislation would infringe on religious liberty and rights of conscience of both religious employers and ordinary business owners. This would be true even if the legislation included the same religious exemptions provided under Title VII.

This is not an issue that should be the subject of federal legislation.

Section 702(a) of Title VII allows religious organizations to discriminate on the basis of religion for "work connected with the carrying on by such corporation, association, educational institution, or society of its activities." But we've already seen that these "exemptions" are not sufficient to protect the fundamental right to freely exercise religion. For example, when a person who professes the same religious beliefs as an employer engages in behavior the organization deems immoral, the employer may at least face costly litigation. In 2005 Professor John Nemecek began appearing on campus as a woman at Spring Arbor University, a Christian liberal arts school. When the university fired him for his behavior, he filed a claim with the Equal Employment Opportunity Commission. The professor asserted that he had not violated a tenet of the university's faith. Although the university should have prevailed if it had litigated the issue, it settled the claim rather than endure costly litigation.

Many Christians exercise their faith through religious ministries—often called "parachurch ministries"—that have even less protection than traditional churches have under these "exceptions." There is a great deal of debate over how closely such a ministry must be connected to a church to qualify for exemption. For example, one court held that a United Methodist children's home was *not* a "religious organization." It made this astonishing ruling despite the fact that the home was hiring a new minister specifically to protect its religions mission. Another court recently devised a nine-part, subjective "balancing" test to decide whether a Jewish community center was "religious" under Title VII. The court said that "not all factors will be relevant in all cases, and the weight given each factor may vary from case to case." Importantly, two of the nine "secularizing" factors identified by the court are very common among parachurch ministries: few such ministries are directly controlled by a church; and many will provide "secular" products (such as food, shelter, counseling, or legal services that are not of themselves religious). That includes organizations like mine, ADF. In sum, many parachurch ministries may not be protected by the Title VII exemptions. That could result in the ministries being forced to hire employees who openly violate the ministries' standards.

Commercial business owners with strong religious views about transsexual issues would have no protection at all under Title VII exemptions. That would be especially problematic for small business owners who are closely associated with the business. In addition to violating the employer's conscience, employing a man who dresses as a woman and wants to use the women's restroom would have a negative impact not only on other employees and customers, but would reflect on the business owner's reputation in the community. It creates an implication that the owner approves of the behavior, or at least accepts the behavior as valid. That is an even bigger issue for owners of day-care centers and religious book stores, where customers have an expectation that their values will be respected.

The Ambiguity of "Gender Identity and Expression"

Gender identity and expression are extremely vague concepts. Gender Public Advocacy Coalition ("GenderPac"), an organization dedicated to eliminating gender norms, defines gender identity as "an individual's self-awareness or fundamental sense of themselves as being masculine or feminine, and male or female." It defines gender expression as "the expression through clothing and behavior that manifests a person's fundamental sense of themselves as masculine or feminine, and male or female. This can include dress, posture, vocal inflection, and so on." In essence, the concept of gender expression is that the totality of the way a person looks, dresses, and acts is his or her gender—in other words, there are an infinite number of genders. Everyone really has their own gender.

Commercial business owners with strong religious views about transsexual issues would have no protection at all.

Typical gender identity provisions prohibit discrimination based upon "actual or perceived" gender identity or expression. This type of provision is highly problematic for employers. How is an employer to know what an employee's actual gender identity is without asking? Could an employer ask without eventually being accused of discrimination? How is one to know how an employer perceives an employee's gender identity or expression? The ultimate subjectivity in gender identity and expression arises from the idea that a person can self-identify his or her gender identity, and this subjective self-identification can change an infinite number of times without notice to the employer. There is simply no objective criteria an employer can utilize to ascertain an employee's gender identity.

The subjective nature of gender identity makes it wholly unlike an objective, immutable characteristic like race. An employer seldom, if ever, needs to wonder whether an employee is African American, Asian, Latino, or Caucasian. He or she can tell by observation. That is impossible with the concept of gender identity. Indeed, gender identity is as unobservable as religion. And religion has never received protection under Title VII without the employee specifically requesting an accommodation of a religious belief. Even then, employers are not generally required to provide the accommodation if it is too inconvenient.

Gender expression is likewise a problematic criterion for employers. How could an employer ever adopt and enforce dress codes if gender expression is a protected category? How is an employer to know whether a person's attire, posture, vocal inflection, and so on really reflects that individual's "fundamental sense of themselves as masculine or feminine, and male or female"? If the totality of the way a person presents oneself is "gender," then gender is the ultimate reason that any employee is disliked. That concept is too subjective and elastic for an employer to know what is required.

Adding gender identity and expression to employment nondiscrimination laws could result in providing special protection for most employees. For example, according to GenderPac, "At some point in their lives, most people experience some form of discrimination or bias as a result of gender stereotyping." Under this view, any employment law prohibiting discrimination based on gender expression or identity may give rise to a significant number of discrimination claims, no matter what an employer does. If "most people" can claim gender identity or expression discrimination when they are terminated from employment, lose out on a promotion, fail to obtain a job, etc., "employment at will" will have lost all meaning.

Gender identity or expression laws have not existed long enough to allow a thorough analysis of how they will be applied. But there have already been lawsuits by transsexuals against employers claiming the right to use restrooms reserved for members of the opposite sex. In fact, eight years ago the Minnesota Court of Appeals ruled that an employer violated an employee's rights by designating restrooms and restroom use on the basis of biological sex. Fortunately, the Minnesota Supreme Court reversed the decision. The Court of Appeals opinion, however, shows how some courts are likely to construe employment laws creating a protected class for gender identity or expression.

The concepts [of transgender discrimination] are far too ambiguous to be susceptible to objective regulations.

Rights of Privacy

Many women in particular are concerned about the infringement on their right to privacy in restrooms if transsexuals with male anatomy are permitted to use women's restrooms. Parents also have a legitimate concern if persons who exercise authority over their children, such as teachers or day care workers, are permitted to use restrooms that are inconsistent with their physical anatomy. The extent of these concerns is evident from recent events in Montgomery County, Maryland, where citizens are attempting to challenge a new gender identity law in a referendum. One of the primary complaints of those challenging the law is that it allows men to use a women's restroom when women and girls are in it. The primary privacy concern is not what happens *after* a transsexual has surgical alteration, but what may happen if physical anatomy is not the criteria for restroom usage. With gender identity being totally subjective, who could challenge any male who says he wants to use a women's restroom? Women and girls should not have to risk having their privacy violated by anatomical males using women's rest rooms.

Given the extent of concern about rights of privacy in restroom usage, employers have a legitimate concern about how to deal with employees who wish to use a restroom designated for members of the opposite sex. The concern is most obvious when a transsexual employee retains his or her original anatomy, but is dressing as a member of the opposite sex. That is the situation that arose in a recent case from Utah, *Etsitty v. Utah Transit Authority*. A man who had been diagnosed with Gender Identity Disorder and had been taking female hormones for nearly 4 years obtained employment as a substitute bus driver. As a bus driver, the employee had to use public restrooms along whatever route he drove. The employee dressed as a man when hired and during orientation, but notified his supervisor of his intent to present himself as a female soon after being hired. While presenting as a woman, the employee began using public restrooms designated for women. When the operations manager learned of the situation, she and a human resources generalist met with the man to inquire about his circumstances. The company ultimately terminated the employee because of concerns about his use of women's restrooms while retaining his male anatomy. The United States Court of Appeals for the Tenth Circuit upheld the termination as valid because gender identity is not covered by Title VII. If gender identity or expression were a protected category, however, the transportation company would have been forced to keep the man as a bus driver. It would have also been forced to face the risk of liability to the public for knowingly allowing a male employee to use public restrooms designated for women.

I strongly urge the committee to reject pressure to extend protected class status to gender identity and expression. The concepts are far too ambiguous to be susceptible to objective regulations that would protect the privacy rights of the public and other employees, or the religious liberty and rights of conscience of religious organizations, parachurch ministries, and commercial employers. "Transgender discrimination" is not an issue that should be the subject of federal legislation.

8

Transgender Children Should Be Accepted

Alan B. Goldberg and Joneil Adriano

Alan B. Goldberg and Joneil Adriano are reporters for ABC News.

From birth, transgender children insist that they were born into the wrong body. What they experience is not just a phase; experts diagnose them with gender identity disorder (GID), the causes of which are unknown. Many are rejected by their families, ostracized by their peers, and grow up hating their own bodies, so children with GID are at high risk of depression, drug abuse, violence, and suicide. One family accepted their male-to-female transgender son, Jazz, and let him make the transition to female: She now wears dresses to school and is known as a girl to everyone. Understanding the doubts, concerns, and experiences faced by such families can further the understanding of transgender children.

From the moment we're born, our gender identity is no secret. We're either a boy or a girl. Gender organizes our world into pink or blue. As we grow up, most of us naturally fit into our gender roles. Girls wear dresses and play with dolls. For boys, it's pants and trucks.

But for some children, what's between their legs doesn't match what's between their ears—they insist they were born into the wrong body. They are transgender children, diagnosed with gender identity disorder, and their parents insist this is not a phase.

"A phase is called a phase because it is just that. It ends. And this is not ending. This is just getting stronger," Renee Jennings told ABC News' Barbara Walters. The Jennings asked that "20/20" not disclose their real name in order to protect the identity of their 6-year old transgender daughter, Jazz.

Most transgender children still live in the shadows, hiding from a world that sees them as freaks of nature. Rejected by their families, many grow up hating their bodies, and fall victim to high rates of depression, drug abuse, violence and suicide.

Today, hundreds of families with transgender children— who have found each other over the Internet—are taking a dramatically different course. They're allowing their children to live in the gender they identify with in order to save them from a future of heartache and pain.

"I think we're a very normal family," said Renee's husband, Scott. "I think we have a very healthy marriage. We love to watch our children in all of their activities, whether it's at school, or on the field playing sports."

"You're Special"

On the surface, the Jennings and their four children are a typical American family. But their youngest child, Jazz, is only in kindergarten, and already she is one of the youngest known cases of an early transition from male to female.

"We'll say things like, 'You're special. God made you special.' Because there aren't very many little girls out there that have a penis," said Renee. "Renee and I are in 100 percent agreement as to how we should raise Jazz," said Scott. "We don't encourage, we support. And we just keep listening to what she tells us."

From the moment he could speak, Jazz made it clear he wanted to wear a dress. At only 15 months, he would unsnap his onesies to make it look like a dress. When his parents praised Jazz as a "good boy," he would correct them, saying he was a good girl.

The Jennings wanted to believe it would pass. Scott said he "was in a bit of denial" about what Jazz was trying to tell them. After all, even their rowdy twin boys, who are two years older than Jazz, had painted their nails growing up. But Jazz kept gravitating to girl things, insisting that his penis was a mistake.

When Jazz was two, he asked his mother a question that left her numb and frozen. "[He] said, 'Mommy, when's the good fairy going to come with her magic wand and change, you know, my genitalia?" according to Renee.

Gender Identity Disorder

Troubled by her son's behavior, Renee eventually consulted her copy of the *Diagnostic and Statistical Manual* or *DSM-IV*, the book used by psychologists and psychiatrists to identify mental disorders. She read the entry for Gender Identity Disorder (GID), with alarming familiarity.

The *DSM-IV* says a diagnosis for GID can be made if: (1) someone has a strong and persistent cross-gender identification; (2) feels a persistent discomfort with his or her sex; (3) this discomfort is not due to being intersex or hermaphroditic; and (4) the discomfort causes significant distress or impairment in their life.

Even Jazz's pediatrician told the Jennings that they had a serious problem on their hands. According to Renee, their doctor said, "'Yes, I believe your child has gender identity disorder, and I recommend that you go to a professional.' And I was—my mouth opened up and you literally had to scrape me off the floor," Renee said.

Dr. Marilyn Volker, a therapist who specializes in sex and gender issues, later confirmed Jazz's diagnosis.

"When we began to talk, and I used—whoops—the pronoun 'he,' I was corrected," Dr. Volker said. Jazz told the therapist, "I'm a girl. I'm she."

No one knows why children like Jazz are transgender— there are only theories.

Dr. Volker then brought out anatomically correct male and female dolls for Jazz to play with, and asked him to point out which one looked like his body. According to Dr. Volker, Jazz pointed to the male doll and said, "This is me now," and then pointed to the female doll and said, "This is what I want."

No Known Cause

No one knows why children like Jazz are transgender—there are only theories. Through the first eight weeks of pregnancy, all fetuses' brains look exactly the same: female, nature's default position.

Only after testosterone surges in the womb do male brains start to develop differently. Some scientists suggest that a hormone imbalance during this stage of development stamped the brains of transgender children with the wrong gender imprint.

With Jazz's diagnosis at hand, the Jennings explained the situation to their other children. In their home, they came to accept Jazz as a girl. There he could wear a dress or dance as a ballerina, although they still referred to Jazz with male pronouns.

In public, they kept Jazz's look more ambiguous or gender neutral, especially at preschool, where he was allowed to put on a pretty top but he had to wear pants. Officially, Jazz remained a boy.

Jazz chafed under that arrangement. He wasn't happy until he could present as a girl both indoors and outdoors. Every day became a struggle, according to Renee. Finally, a dance recital opened the Jennings' eyes to just how unhappy Jazz was.

The Turning Point

"She wasn't allowed to wear a tutu, like the rest of the girls. And she just kind of stood there and snapped her finger and did the tapping thing with the toe, and just looked so sad," Renee recalled. "It was heartbreaking to watch. Really heartbreaking."

She is a boy but she wants to be a girl, so we let her wear a bathing suit.

The dance recital was a turning point. The Jennings then made the difficult decision to let their son become their daughter. On his fifth birthday, Jazz wore a girl's one-piece bathing suit. "He" was now "she," and an innocent pool party became a "coming out" to all of her friends.

"They referred to her as a boy. But kids are very accepting at that age. They believe what you tell them. She is a boy but she wants to be a girl, so we let her wear a bathing suit," said Renee.

"That was the first time in front of everybody, she . . . announced to the world, that she was a girl," Scott added.

Living as a Girl

So how does a 5-year-old biological boy begin living as a girl? For Jazz, it meant growing her hair out, piercing her ears, and wearing dresses everywhere—even to kindergarten.

At school, Jazz is registered as a boy. Her teachers know she's biologically male, but most of her classmates don't. She's lucky because there's a unisex bathroom and in sports, unisex teams. But even play dates are an issue.

Renee said, "I don't want to send Jazz over to anybody's house unless they know the truth. Nor will I let a child walk into our house, and play with Jazz, unless it's been explained to them."

Jazz's physical safety is always on Scott's mind. He worries about teasing, taunting, or worse. "Every day I'm afraid that I might get a call that something happened. But what we've tried to do for Jazz is give her as much self-esteem as we can. We have older brothers, and an older sister, that are always looking out for her. Keeping their eyes on her."

Dresses and Mermaids

After months of careful deliberation, the Jennings agreed to participate in Barbara Walters' special on transgender children, in the hope that doing so would further understanding of Jazz and others like her.

"I don't feel like you can capture the true essence of a child like Jazz until you see her in her environment doing things that she would normally do. It makes it a lot more believable," said Scott.

Jazz's bedroom is filled with things one would find in a typical girl's room: dresses in the closet, pink and purple sheets, and a bed overflowing with stuffed animals. There are also mermaids—lots and lots of mermaids.

Asked why she liked mermaids so much, Jazz said, "Because they're different than us." She added, "They have tails."

"All of the male to female younger transgender children are obsessed with mermaids," said Renee. "It's because of the ambiguous genitalia. There's nothing below the waist but a tail. And how appealing is that for somebody who doesn't like what's down there?"

Jazz told Walters that she was very happy being a girl, and that she always thought of herself as one. When people ask her whether she's a boy or a girl, Jazz answers without any hesitation: a girl.

Jazz also showed Walters a drawing of a little girl with a tear-streaked face. Jazz drew it when she was in pre-school and still dressing as a boy. Asked by Walters why the little girl was crying, Jazz said, "Because she wants to wear the dress to school."

Now allowed to wear a dress, Renee reports that Jazz enjoys going to school and has lots of friends. If Jazz hadn't been allowed to transition, Renee said, Jazz today would be "very depressed" and "suffering."

Underneath her frilly dresses, [Jazz] still has the body of a boy, and puberty looms large over the horizon.

The Child That Never Was

For all intents and purposes, Jazz is a girl. But underneath her frilly dresses, she still has the body of a boy, and puberty looms large over the horizon.

"This child will come into my bedroom in the middle of the night, [and say] 'Mommy, mommy, I had a bad dream that I had a beard and moustache like daddy, and I don't ever want to have a beard or a moustache,'" Renee said.

In order to prevent Jazz's nightmare from becoming a reality, the Jennings will probably allow her to undergo hormone therapy when she reaches puberty. First, Jazz's doctor will prescribe blockers that will stop her from growing body hair and developing other masculine characteristics.

A few years after beginning that regimen, Jazz will start taking estrogen, which will allow her body to go through a form of female puberty. She will grow breasts and her body fat will move to her hips. Most doctors will not perform sex reassignment surgery until the age of consent, 18. The Jennings say that if Jazz chooses to also take that step, they will fully support her. But they are also mindful of keeping all of Jazz's options open.

"We check in with her all the time," Renee said. "I tell her, I say, 'Jazz, if you ever feel like you want to dress like a boy again, cut your hair, you just let me know.' And she goes, 'Mommy, why would I want to do that?'"

While Jazz's parents now fully accept their son as their daughter, the transition has not been without considerable doubt and stress. Many parents grieve for the child that never was. "I mourn the loss of the idea of my son," Renee said. "I see pictures and the video, and that child's gone. But there's a wonderful person now that's with us."

By any measure, the Jennings home is a happy place. Kids play, kids fight. For now, Jazz lives safely inside a bubble, but the enormity of Jazz's situation is not lost on her parents.

"I always say that I'm in the front line. Jazz is protected, because she's not getting the slack, because I am putting out the fires before they burn her," said Renee. "I want to pave the way for a better life for her, and any trans kids. They didn't ask to be born this way."

9

Children's Sex and Gender Should Not Be Reassigned

Gail Besse

Gail Besse is a writer based in Boston, Massachusetts.

Instead of psychiatric treatment, disturbed children who suppos-edly identify as the opposite sex are being provided hormones that have a profound effect on their bodies. "Transgender" pa-tients as young as ten years old are given drugs to postpone pu-berty and hormones to change their physical differences from one gender to the other. However, maleness and femaleness cannot be altered. No scientific evidence supports the existence of gender dysphoria, and the defining of these children as "transgender" and reassigning of their sex feeds into a culture of self-absorption and dysfunction.

A clinic at [Boston] Children's Hospital is providing pow-erful hormones to disturbed children who believe they should have been born the opposite sex.

The Gender Management Service Clinic helps youngsters with real physical problems, but it also treats those "with no known anatomic or biochemical disorder who feel like a mem-ber of the opposite sex," according to its website.

These patients are called "transgender," a term coined by homosexual activists pushing the idea that "gender" is a changeable psychological notion divorced from biology. The American Psychiatric Association calls the condition Gender Identity Disorder.

Gail Besse, "'Sex-change' Treatment for 'Transgender' Kids? Hospital Clinic Draw Moral Criticism," *The Anchor*, May 8, 2008. Reproduced by permission.

Children as young as 10 years old are given drugs to delay puberty, then if they continue "treatment," stronger hormones like testosterone and estrogen to change their physical characteristics, according to a March 30 [2008] *Boston Sunday Globe* article. If they then opt for surgical mutation, this would be done elsewhere.

The clinic, which the hospital calls "unique in the Western Hemisphere," opened last year but received a shot of free advertising with the highly sympathetic *Globe* report.

In that article, pediatric endocrinologist Dr. Norman Spack, who runs the clinic with urologist Dr. David Diamond, explained that the hormone procedure will likely make the young people infertile.

The evidence shows that in a boy, he's over-identified with his mother or other female to the extent that his ego boundaries are blurred.

"Cooperating with Psychosis"

The following case history is detailed on the Children's Hospital website. Four years ago, Holly Earle of Vermont was depressed and confused at the progression of puberty. The 14-year-old convinced her parents that although born a girl, she was a "trans" who should be a boy.

The family eventually turned to Spack, who prescribed testosterone, which stopped menstruation and gave Holly facial hair and a deeper voice. Holly bound her breasts to conceal them until she could have a double mastectomy, which was carried out at another hospital.

Holly had her name legally changed to Hal. As of last year, Hal was considering a hysterectomy in the future, and was now "presenting" as a male.

"This is cooperating with psychosis," commented moral theologian Father Anthony Mastroeni of Patterson, N.J. Father

Mastroeni, who has taught at Franciscan University of Steubenville and Christendom College, has written extensively to refute the notion that sex-change surgery might be morally justified.

"It does nothing but increase human misery," he said in an interview. "There's no scientific evidence that anyone is born with gender dysphoria."

There are legitimate medical problems, such as ambiguous genitalia, that doctors can correct, he said. "But when there's nothing to suggest that these kids have a genetic anomaly, something in their background is dysfunctional. The evidence shows that in a boy, he's over-identified with his mother or other female to the extent that his ego boundaries are blurred. With a girl, usually her mother was seen as ineffective and she identified with a dominant father figure."

Spack could not be reached for comment. He recently testified before the Massachusetts Legislature in favor of a proposed Transgender Rights and Hate Crimes Bill, which was defeated but which gay activists hope to resurrect.

'Sex-Reassignment' Damage

The clinic's Web page links to various groups pushing to redefine sexuality: for example, the Human Rights Campaign ("Working for gay, lesbian, bisexual and transgender equal rights"), and the Transkids Purple Rainbow Foundation ("Our kids aren't pink or blue, but various shades of purple.")

Medical schools actually stopped encouraging sex changes decades ago.

Pro-family and pro-life groups, appalled that the world-renowned center for children's health care is condoning this procedure, picked up the news. In April the story was further publicized by MassResistance.org, a Waltham [Massachusetts]-

based family organization, and then by *LifeSiteNews.com* and *OneNewsNow.com*, a publication of the American Family News Network.

Hospital spokesman James Newton declined to comment on whether recent publicity has generated public feedback. He also declined to say whether the hormone therapy is intended to prepare youngsters for surgery elsewhere. "The only information I can offer at this time is what is available on our Web site," he said.

Although the site states that medical experience with transgenderism is "limited," evidently Johns Hopkins University and other medical schools actually stopped encouraging sex changes decades ago.

"I have witnessed a great deal of damage from sex-reassignment," wrote Dr. Paul McHugh, University Distinguished Service Professor of Psychiatry at Johns Hopkins, in his 2004 *First Things* article, "Surgical Sex."

"We psychiatrists, I thought, would do better to concentrate on trying to fix their minds and not their genitalia," McHugh said he eventually concluded of his patients who thought themselves transsexual.

"As for the adults who came to us claiming to have discovered their 'true' sexual identity and to have heard about sex-change operations, we psychiatrists have been distracted from studying the causes and natures of their mental misdirections by preparing them for surgery and for a life in the other sex," he added. "We have wasted scientific and technical resources and damaged our professional credibility by collaborating with madness rather than trying to study, cure, and ultimately prevent it."

Sex Unchangeable

Father Mastroeni placed the scenario in a societal context. "We're living in an age of narcissism, of flight from struggling or pain, with an obsessive-compulsive focus on pleasure. Children become confirmed in their narcissism when they watch self-absorbed parents. So they insist they want to 'free themselves' from this dysfunctional idea they have of themselves. That grown people would sanction feeding this neurosis is even sadder."

The Vatican's Congregation of the Doctrine of the Faith in 2000 issued a document that authoritatively concluded "sex-change" operations are invalid—they do not change a person's sex, according to a *Catholic News Service* report reprinted in *LifeSiteNews.com.*

In its brochure "A Gender Identity Disorder Goes Mainstream," the Traditional Values Coalition states: "In reality, no person can actually change into a different sex. Maleness and femaleness are in the DNA and are unchangeable."

10

Sex Reassignment Surgery Is a Medical Necessity

World Professional Association for Transgender Health, Inc.

The World Professional Association for Transgender Health, Inc., (WPATH) is an international organization dedicated to understanding and providing treatment to individuals with gender identity disorders.

Sex-reassignment surgery is essential to the well-being of people with gender identity disorder (GID). Along with hormone treatment, nongenital surgeries—such as mastectomies in female-to-male transsexuals and breast augmentation for male-to-female transsexuals—greatly improve their quality of life and self-image. These medical procedures have existed for decades, and many studies demonstrate that sex-reassignment surgery is effective. Consequently, health insurance carriers and health care providers are urged to not exclude from coverage transgender people or medically prescribed treatments for making the transition to another gender. In addition, it is unethical to deny transgender people treatment based on HIV or hepatitis status.

The World Professional Association for Transgender Health (WPATH) is an international association devoted to the understanding and treatment of individuals with gender identity disorders. Founded in 1979, and currently with over 300 physician, psychologist, social scientist, and legal professional members, all of whom are engaged in research and/or clinical

World Professional Association for Transgender Health, Inc., "WPATH Clarification on Medical Necessity of Treatment, Sex Reassignment, and Insurance Coverage in the U.S.A.," June 17, 2008. Reproduced by permission.

practice that affects the lives of transgender and transsexual people, WPATH is the oldest interdisciplinary professional association in the world concerned with this specialty.

Gender Identity Disorder (GID), more commonly known as transsexualism, is a condition recognized in the *Diagnostic and Statistical Manual of Mental Disorders*, (*DSM-IV*, 1994, and *DSM-IV-TR*, 2000), published by the American Psychiatric Association. Transsexualism is also recognized in the *International Statistical Classification of Diseases and Related Health Problems*, Ninth Revision, published by the World Health Organization, for which the United States is a signatory. The criteria listed for GID are descriptive of many people who experience dissonance between their sex as assigned at birth and their gender identity, which is developed in early childhood and understood to be firmly established by age 4, though for some transgender individuals, gender identity may remain somewhat fluid for many years. The *DSM-IV* descriptive criteria were developed to aid in diagnosis and treatment to alleviate the clinically significant distress and impairment known as gender dysphoria that is often associated with transsexualism.

The WPATH Standards of Care for Gender Identity Disorders were first issued in 1979, and articulate the "professional consensus about the psychiatric, psychological, medical and surgical management of GID." Periodically revised to reflect the latest clinical practice and scientific research, the Standards also unequivocally reflect this Association's conclusion that treatment is medically necessary. Medical necessity is a term common to health care coverage and insurance policies in the United States, and a common definition among insurers is:

> "[H]ealth care services that a Physician, exercising prudent clinical judgment, would provide to a patient for the purpose of preventing, evaluating, diagnosing or treating an illness, injury, disease or its symptoms, and that are: (a) in accordance with generally accepted standards of medical

practice; (b) clinically appropriate, in terms of type, frequency, extent, site and duration, and considered effective for the patient's illness, injury, or disease; and (c) not primarily for the convenience of the patient, physician, or other health care provider, and not more costly than an alternative service or sequence of services at least as likely to produce equivalent therapeutic or diagnostic results as to the diagnosis or treatment of that patient's illness, injury or disease."

"Generally accepted standards of medical practice means standards that are based on credible scientific evidence published in peer-reviewed medical literature generally recognized by the relevant medical community, Physician Specialty Society recommendations and the views of Physicians practicing in relevant clinical areas and any other relevant factors."

The current Board of Directors of the WPATH herewith expresses its conviction that sex reassignment, properly indicated and performed as provided by the Standards of Care, has proven to be beneficial and effective in the treatment of individuals with transsexualism, gender identity disorder, and/or gender dysphoria. Sex reassignment plays an undisputed role in contributing toward favorable outcomes, and comprises Real Life Experience, legal name and sex change on identity documents, as well as medically necessary hormone treatment, counseling, psychotherapy, and other medical procedures. Genital reconstruction is not required for social gender recognition, and such surgery should not be a prerequisite for document or record changes; the Real Life Experience component of the transition process is crucial to psychological adjustment, and is usually completed prior to any genital reconstruction, when appropriate for the patient, according to the WPATH Standards of Care. Changes to documentation are important aids to social functioning, and are a necessary component of the pre-surgical process; delay of document changes may have a deleterious impact on a patient's social integration and personal safety.

Medically necessary sex reassignment procedures also include complete hysterectomy [removal of female reproductive organs], bilateral mastectomy [removal of both breasts], chest reconstruction or augmentation as appropriate to each patient (including breast prostheses [artificial replacements] if necessary), genital reconstruction (by various techniques which must be appropriate to each patient, including, for example, skin flap hair removal, penile and testicular prostheses, as necessary), facial hair removal, and certain facial plastic reconstruction as appropriate to the patient. . . .

Furthermore, not every patient will have a medical need for identical procedures; clinically appropriate treatments must be determined on an individualized basis with the patient's physician.

Sex reassignment plays an undisputed role in contributing toward favorable outcomes.

The medical procedures attendant to sex reassignment are not "cosmetic" or "elective" or for the mere convenience of the patient. These reconstructive procedures are not optional in any meaningful sense, but are understood to be medically necessary for the treatment of the diagnosed condition. Further, the WPATH Standards consider it unethical to deny eligibility for sex reassignment surgeries or hormonal therapies solely on the basis of blood seropositivity for infections such as HIV or hepatitis.

These medical procedures and treatment protocols are not experimental: decades of both clinical experience and medical research show they are essential to achieving well-being for the transsexual patient. For example, a recent study of female-to-male transsexuals found significantly improved quality of life following cross-gender hormonal therapy. Moreover, those who had also undergone chest reconstruction had significantly higher scores for general health, social functioning, as well as mental health. . . .

Available routinely in the United States and in many other countries, these treatments are cost effective rather than cost prohibitive. In the United States, numerous large employers (e.g., City and County of San Francisco, University of California, University of Michigan, IBM, etc.) have negotiated contracts with their insurance carriers to enable medically necessary treatment for transsexualism and/or GID to be provided to covered individuals. As more carriers realize the validity and effectiveness of treatment (Aetna, Cigna, and others now have protocols), coverage is being offered, increasingly at no additional premium cost. . . .

The medical procedures attendant to sex reassignment are not "cosmetic" or "elective" or for the mere convenience of the patient.

The WPATH Board of Directors urges health insurance carriers and healthcare providers in the United States to eliminate transgender or trans-sex exclusions and to provide coverage for transgender patients and the medically prescribed sex reassignment services necessary for their treatment and wellbeing, and to ensure that their ongoing healthcare (both routine and specialized) is readily accessible.

11

Sex Reassignment Surgery Is Not a Medical Necessity

John Rohan

John Rohan is a U.S. Intelligence Army officer based in South Korea.

Sex-change operations are not a medical necessity, and such surgeries waste resources and tax dollars. For instance, a gender-disordered prisoner's lawsuit to have his procedures paid for by the state of Massachusetts cost $58,000 for expert eye witnesses, not including court costs and legal fees. Also, transgender activists have sued states that refused to provide free sex-change operations to prisoners and government workers. And the situation is worse in other countries, in which tattoo removal and birth certificate changes were enforced for transgender people. The fact is, however, that no amount of surgery or hormone therapy can change a person's sex.

Michelle Kosilek (who legally changed his first name from "Robert" in 1993) is currently serving a life sentence in Massachusetts for killing his wife back in 1990. As you may have guessed from the name change, he would also like to have a sex change, which is now known by the more PC [politically correct] term: "sex reassignment surgery". He and some sympathetic doctors are claiming that he needs it to cure his depression and are demanding that it be provided by

John Rohan, "Americans: Your Tax Dollars at Work Toward Sex Change Operations," Shield of Achilles, June 28, 2007. Reproduced by permission of the author. Article was originally published with hyperlinks and can be accessed online at http://www.shieldofachilles.net/2007/06/americans-your-tax-dollars-at-work.html

the state. Naturally, the Massachusetts Department of Corrections refused. So Mr. Kosilek filed a lawsuit. More than one, actually. Right now a judge is deliberating over his third request.

Wasted Tax Dollars and Time

So the judge hasn't ruled and Kosilek hasn't gotten his sex change yet. So why does the headline say that tax dollars were supporting this?

Here's why—the charges for 10 medical expert witnesses alone in this farce so far have totalled $58,000, and that doesn't count court costs, attorney fees, Department of Correction fees, and of course, all the wasted time over this nonsense. Oh, and by the way—this is Kosilek's second lawsuit and third time in court over this issue.

The chance of the judge ruling favorably to Mr. Kosilek is very slim, and even if he did, the chances of it surviving an inevitable appeal are slimmer yet. Still, why on Earth did it even come this far? As one commenter in *Newsday* put it:

> This 'case' shouldn't have gotten beyond the guard at the jail laughing when the prisoner asked. It should never have become anything more than an inside joke at the prison.

Incidentally, that *Newsday* article reads more than just a little friendly to the plaintiff. They point out that the money spent so far on fighting this action is far more than it would cost to give him the sex change (about $20,000), without adding in the fact that the real worry here is setting a precedent that will oblige the State to provide all kinds of elective procedures in the future. What's next, Nose jobs? Breast implants? Viagra? Hair transplants for the balding? As of right now, 10 inmates in Massachusetts are receiving hormone therapy, and two have already requested to get the surgery as well.

Some people seem to think all of the above:

But advocates say in some cases—such as that of Kosilek, who has twice attempted suicide—sex-change surgery is as much a medical necessity as treatment for diabetes or high blood pressure.

"The duty belongs to the prison to figure out how to fulfill its constitutional obligations to both provide adequate medical care and provide a fundamental security for all inmates," said Cole Thaler, an attorney with Lambda Legal, a gay- and transgender-rights group.

[Sex-change operations] require numerous psychiatric visits, hormone therapy, and doctors visits, all of which drain time and resources . . . which should instead be reserved for people who are really sick.

So the prison can be forced to do an inmate's bidding over suicide threats? And has anyone considered the possibility of Mr. Kosilek paying for this operation himself?

Overlawyered.com (with some great comments) pointed out *Newsday*'s little disclaimer at the end of the article:

This version CORRECTS 'himself' to 'herself.'

Not only is this PC pandering at its worst, it is also incorrect, since Mr. Kosilek has not yet had the surgery and is still legally a man.

And there are other issues to hear besides money. Sex change operations aren't just done overnight. They require numerous psychiatric visits, hormone therapy, and doctors visits, all of which drain time and resources escorting this man to his appointments or providing medication which should instead be reserved for people who are really sick. Add to this the security problems during the procedure of having a man/woman in either a man's prison or woman's prison.

Massachusetts is not the only place that has struggled over this issue. Last year [in 2006], Wisconsin's legislature tried to ban such surgeries and hormone therapies from their prisons, only to be sued by the ACLU [American Civil Liberties Union]. Several years ago, San Francisco decided to grant free sex-changes to city employees, and was not sued, since that city is rather on the fringe of American life.

An Illusion Only

But if you think this is ridiculous, just remember it could be worse. Take the UK [United Kingdom] for example. The NHS (National Health Service) in Britain has provided these operations for free (well not exactly free, but through public funds) since 1998, apparently even to jailed persons. Incredibly, even after paying for one such sex change on a 57-year-old man, they also agreed to pay thousands of pounds worth of tattoo removal for him/her, because the tattoos were "unladylike" (never mind the fact that tattoos are very popular with women—that is, *real* women—all across Europe). This is not only nuts but terribly unfair, because, if the commenters are to be believed, the NHS will not fund tattoo removal for ordinary persons. And it gets even worse: in 2002, the UK was also forced by the European Court of Human Rights to allow transgendered persons to change their birth certificates. The reason is many need these certificates to get married in countries where same-sex marriages are illegal. But the problem is, this completely defies common sense. The sex you were born with is a medical fact, and you can't change the past with the stroke of a pen.

As a side note, believe it or not, these surgeries are legal in Iran, although not on the government's dime. At least one man-turned-woman had second thoughts after being forced to comply with Iran's restrictions on women.

One more thing. I hate to break it to many of these "experts" but sex-reassignment surgery does not actually turn a man into a woman, or vice versa. All it can do is make a person superficially appear as another gender, and changes their legal status on paper. But this is an illusion only. It does not change DNA or hormones (which must be supplied for life) and it does not allow a person to ever have children as a member of the new gender.

12

Schools Are Unprepared to Accommodate Transgender Athletes

Pat Griffin and Helen Carroll

Pat Griffin is director of It Takes a Team!, a project of the Women's Sports Foundation that aims to end homophobia in athletics. Helen Carroll is director of the National Center for Lesbian Rights Sports Project.

Transgender student athletes face misconceptions and prejudice and most high schools, colleges, and universities do not have policies and practices in athletics for gender identity and expression. Most sports programs are divided by sex. Determining whether a transgender student plays for a men's or women's team—along with what pronoun or which locker rooms to use— becomes confusing and frustrating. These students deserve full inclusion in sports, and policies and practices must address their medical eligibility to play in men's or women's divisions, adhere to discrimination laws, evaluate concerns of "unfair advantage" in the performance of transgender athletes, and educate sports administration and staff.

> "I was really worried about coming out as transgender to anyone else because I knew there weren't any policies. I was so afraid that my school would ban me from my sport and that was the only thing I had at the time. I finally decided to come out my senior year of college because I was going down a slippery slope and I didn't think I could pull myself out if I didn't come out."
>
> *—A transgender former college athlete*

Pat Griffin and Helen Carroll, "The Transgender Athlete," *Inside Higher Ed*, January 25, 2010. Reproduced by permission of the authors.

Many transgender athletes relate similar experiences that make their participation on college teams painful and frustrating: An athlete is called "she/he" and "it" by opposing players during a game. An athlete stops playing sports in college because it becomes too uncomfortable to use the locker room. An athlete has to change clothes in a utility closet separate from the rest of the team. An athlete quits the team because it becomes too painful to keep reminding coaches and teammates about the athlete's preferred pronouns. None of the institutions or athletic conferences in which these athletes compete have a policy governing the inclusion of transgender student-athletes on sports teams.

These descriptions and many others like them characterize the experiences of many young people who identify as transgender and want to play on their colleges' athletic teams. Transgender is a broad term used to describe the experiences of people whose gender identity and expression do not match the sex they were assigned at birth. Some people transition to live as their preferred gender by changing their names and the pronouns they use to refer to themselves. They express their preferred gender through choice of clothes, hairstyles and other manifestations of gender expression and identity. Some transgender people undergo reconstructive surgery or take hormones to make their bodies more congruent with their internal sense of themselves. Others do not.

Since the increased visibility of a transgender rights movement in the 1980s and a school-based LGBT [lesbian, gay, bisexual, and transgender] "safe schools" movement in the 1990s, more young people have the language and information they need to identify the gender dissonance they experience between the sex they were assigned at birth and the gender identity that they know to be true for them. They are increasingly identifying themselves as transgender and they are doing it at earlier ages. In addition, parents are much more likely to support their transgender children and advocate for them in schools. As more states add "gender identity and expression" to non-discrimination legislation and as these legal protections are applied to schools, transgender students and their parents have increased leverage to ensure that educational institutions address their needs. K-12 school and college educators find themselves playing catch up as they learn to accommodate the educational needs of trans-identified students and protect them from bullying and harassment in school or at college.

Schools and Colleges Are Unprepared

Many of these young people want to play on their schools' or colleges' sports teams. As a result, athletic directors and coaches increasingly find themselves unprepared to make decisions about what team a transgender student is eligible to play for. As the number of transgender students who want to play on school sports teams increases, school athletic leaders must identify effective and fair policies to ensure their right to participate. Though the issue of accommodating the needs of transgender students, staff and faculty in higher education has received attention, it has not been adequately addressed in athletics. Many colleges have changed policies on access to bathrooms, residence halls or face controversy because they have not done so. In athletics, conversations about accommodating transgender students have only recently begun.

For the most part, athletic teams at high schools and colleges are segregated by sex and divided into men's and women's teams. For transgender students, determining on which gender's team, if any, they will be allowed to play can be a difficult process fraught with misconceptions, ignorance and discrimination. Few high school or collegiate athletic programs, administrators or coaches are prepared to address a transgender student's interest in participating in athletics in a systematic, fair and effective manner. Few athletes have been given the information that would prepare them to participate on a team with a teammate whose gender identity is different from the sex they were assigned at birth.

The vast majority of school athletic programs have no policy governing the inclusion of transgender athletes and athletic staff have no idea how to accommodate a transgender student who wants to play on a college sports team. Even basic accommodations can be confusing, such as what pronouns or name to use to refer to that student, where that student should change clothes for practice or competition, what bathroom that student should use, or how to apply team dress codes.

Athletic directors and coaches increasingly find themselves unprepared to make decisions about what team a transgender student is eligible to play for.

Washington is the only state that has a policy identifying the process for enabling transgender students to participate in high school athletics. The National Collegiate Athletic Association [NCAA] does not prohibit transgender students from participating in NCAA sponsored events, but recommends that NCAA member institutions use a student's official identity documents (birth certificate, driver's license or passport) to determine whether a student-athlete is eligible to compete on the men's or women's team. Because of wide variations in state requirements for changing identity documents, however, the NCAA recommendation unintentionally creates an inequitable situation depending on where the student is enrolled.

Applying the 2004 International Olympic Committee [IOC] policy governing the participation of transsexual athletes in IOC sanctioned events to collegiate athletics is problematic for a number of reasons. The IOC policy, though pioneering, is criticized by knowledgeable medical experts and transgender advocates for requiring genital reconstructive surgery as a criterion for eligibility. Moreover, applying the IOC policy to collegiate sports does not take into account the eligibility limits placed on individual athletes or the age and developmental needs of this age group.

Developing Sound Policies and Practices

After a number of informal discussions with collegiate athletic leaders and transgender students who want to participate in sports, the National Center for Lesbian Rights Sports Project and the Women's Sports Foundation initiative, It Takes A Team!, joined forces to organize a national meeting on these topics in the fall [2009]. Two of the guiding principles for the discussion were 1) Participation in interscholastic and intercollegiate athletics is a valuable part of the education experience for all students and 2) Transgender student-athletes should have equal opportunity to participate in sports.

The 40 participants, including representatives from the NCAA and Interscholastic High School Athletic Association leaders, were an impressive group of experts from a range of disciplines—law, medicine, sports, advocacy, and athletics—all of whom share an interest in transgender issues. The goals were to identify best practices and develop model policies for high school and collegiate athletic leaders to ensure the full inclusion of transgender student-athletes. A report will be issued in 2010 outlining specific recommendations for high school and collegiate athletic programs.

Specific issues discussed included:

- From a medical perspective, what are the salient factors that should be used to determine for which team (women's or men's) a transgender student is eligible to participate?

- From a policy and school regulation perspective, how can we develop policies governing the participation of transgender students in athletics that adhere to state and federal laws protecting students from discrimination based on gender identity and expression?

- From an athletic perspective, how can we address concerns about "competitive equity" or "unfair advantage" while acknowledging the broad diversity of performance already exhibited within both women's and men's sports?

- From an education perspective, how can we ensure that athletic administrators, staff, parents of athletes and student-athletes have access to sound and effective education related to the participation of transgender students in athletics? . . .

Transgender student-athletes should have equal opportunity to participate in sports.

The most powerful information came from the transgender student-athletes in attendance, who detailed their challenges and triumphs and the importance of high school and collegiate sport participation. Their stories reinforced the necessity of developing sound policies and practices that enable transgender student-athletes to play the sports they love in an environment where their gender identity and expression are accepted as one more aspect of the diversity typical of school and college sports teams.

Organizations to Contact

The editors have compiled the following list of organizations concerned with the issues debated in this book. The descriptions are derived from materials provided by the organizations. All have publications or information available for interested readers. The list was compiled on the date of publication of the present volume; names, addresses, phone and fax numbers, and e-mail and Internet addresses may change. Be aware that many organizations take several weeks or longer to respond to inquiries, so allow as much time as possible.

American Civil Liberties Union (ACLU)
125 Broad St., 18th Floor, New York, NY   10004
(212) 549-2500
Web site: www.aclu.org

The ACLU is the nation's oldest and largest civil liberties organization, and it works for the rights of transgender people. Relevant ACLU publications include "Know Your Rights—Transgender People and the Law," its annual "Transgender Docket," as well as an online newsletter, *ACLU Online*.

Concerned Women for America (CWFA)
1015 15th St. NW, Suite 1100, Washington, DC   20005
(202) 488-7000 • fax: (202) 488-0806
e-mail: mail@cwfa.org
Web site: www.cwfa.org

CWFA is an educational and legal defense foundation that seeks to strengthen the traditional family by promoting Judeo-Christian moral standards. It argues against the granting of additional civil rights protections to transgender people. The CWFA publishes the monthly magazine *Family Voice* and various public policy articles about sexuality.

Family Research Council (FRC)

801 G St. NW, Washington, DC 20005

(202) 393-2100 • fax: (202) 393-2134

Web site: www.frc.org

FRC is a research, resource, and educational organization that promotes the traditional family, which the council defines as a group of people bound by marriage, blood, or adoption. The council opposes the transgender rights movement and scrutinizes gender identity and expression laws. FRC also hosts a weekly radio show, *Washington Watch Radio*.

Focus on the Family

8605 Explorer Dr., Colorado Springs, CO 80920

(800) 232-6459 • fax: (719) 531-5181

Web site: www.focusonthefamily.org

Focus on the Family is a conservative Christian organization that promotes traditional family values and gender roles. Its publications include the monthly magazine *Focus on the Family* and articles regarding gender identity politics and transgender rights and lifestyles.

Human Rights Campaign (HRC)

1640 Rhode Island Ave., Washington, DC 20036-3276

(202) 628-4160 • fax: (202) 347-5323

Web site: www.hrc.org

HRC provides information about national political issues affecting lesbian, gay, bisexual, and transgender (LGBT) Americans. It offers resources to educate congressional leaders and the public on critical issues such as ending workplace discrimination, combating hate crimes, protecting LGBT families, and working to better the understanding of transgender people. HRC publishes *Equality* and *LAWbriefs*.

Traditional Values Coalition (TVC)

139 C St. SE, Washington, DC 20003

(202) 547-8570 • fax: (202) 546-6403

e-mail: mail@traditionalvalues.org
Web site: www.traditionalvalues.org

Founded in 1980, TVC is the largest non-denominational, grassroots church lobby in America. The coalition, which speaks on behalf of more than 43,000 churches, bridges racial and socioeconomic barriers and includes most Christian denominations. With an emphasis on the restoration of traditional values, TVC focuses on such issues as religious liberties and what it sees as the lesbian, gay, bisexual, and transgender (LGBT) agenda.

TransYouth Family Allies (TYFA)

PO Box 1471, Holland, MI   49422-1471
(888) 462-8932
e-mail: info@imatyfa.org
Web site: www.imatyfa.org

TYFA works to empower children and families by partnering with educators, service providers, and communities to develop supportive environments in which gender may be expressed and respected. It envisions a society free of suicide and violence in which all children are respected and celebrated. TYFA provides resources for parents, children, teachers, and health care professionals.

World Professional Association for Transgender Health (WPATH)

1300 S Second St., Suite 180, Minneapolis, MN   55454
e-mail: wpath@wpath.org
Web site: www.wpath.org

Formerly known as the Harry Benjamin International Gender Dysphoria Association, WPATH is an international multidisciplinary professional association. The mission of WPATH is to promote evidence-based care, education, research, advocacy, public policy, and respect in transgender health. It holds a biennial symposium and publishes *WPATH Standards of Care*.

Bibliography

Books

Cris Beam	*Transparent: Love, Family, and Living the T with Transgender Teenagers.* Orlando, FL: Hartcourt Books, 2007.
Michael Brinkle	*Return to Michael: A Transgender Story.* Lincoln, NE: iUniverse, 2006.
Lori B. Girshick	*Transgender Voices: Beyond Men and Women.* Lebanon, NH: University Press of New England, 2008.
Joann Herman	*Transgender Explained.* Bloomington, IN: AuthorHouse, 2009.
Kimberly Hyatt-Wallace	*The Transgender Myth.* Raleigh, NC: Lulu, 2004.
David L. Rowland and Luca Incrocci	*Handbook of Sexual and Gender Identity Disorders.* Hoboken, NJ: John Wiley & Sons, 2008.
Arlene Stein	*Shameless: Sexual Dissidence in American Culture.* New York: NYU Press, 2006.
Susan Stryker	*Transgender History.* Berkeley, CA: Seal Press, 2008.

Periodicals

Jacob Anderson	"Out of Bounds," *Bitch*, May 28, 2008.

Alice Dreger   "The Sex of Athletes: One Issue, Many Variables," *New York Times*, October 24, 2009.

Selwyn Duke   "Death of the West: Our Sexual Identity Crisis," NewsWithViews.com, September 29, 2009.

Laura Fitzpatrick   "The Gender Conundrum," *Time*, November 8, 2007.

Sharon Gaughan   "What About Non-Op Transsexuals? A No-Op Notion," TS-Si.org, August 18, 2006.

Stephanie Grant   "Transgender Children: Frequently Asked Questions," www.abcnews.go.com, April 25, 2007.

Jeff Jacoby   "Pregnant, Yes—But Not a Man," *Boston Globe*, April 13, 2008.

Les Kinsolving   "What Next? Transgender Showers for Kids," *World Net Daily*, April 19, 2010.

Marc Lostracco   "But for Today I Am a Boy," *Torontoist*, May 9, 2008.

Julia Reischel   "See Dick Be Jane," *Broward-Palm Beach New Times*, May 18, 2006.

Thomas Rogers   "What the Pregnant Man Didn't Deliver," *Salon*, July 3, 2008.

Hanna Rosin   "A Boy's Life," *Atlantic*, November 2008.

William Saletan   "Trans Figure," *Slate*, February 16,
                       2010.

Lois Wingerson   "Gender Identity Disorder: Has
                      Accepted Practice Caused Harm?"
                      Psychiatric Times, May 19, 2009.

Index